AILA Review

Linguistic inequality in
scientific communication today

VOLUME 20 2007

Guest Editors Augusto Carli
Università di Modena-Reggio Emilia
Ulrich Ammon
Universität Duisburg-Essen

Editor Jasone Cenoz
University of the Basque Country

Editorial Board Ulrich Ammon
Universität Duisburg-Essen, Germany
Maria Antonieta Alba Celani
National Research Council, Brazil
Roy Lyster
McGill University
Howard Nicholas
La Trobe University, Australia

John Benjamins Publishing Company
Amsterdam/Philadelphia

Table of contents

Introduction

Augusto Carli and Ulrich Ammon
Università degli Studi di Modena-Reggio Emilia, Italy / Universität
Duisburg-Essen, Germany

Almost half a century after the foundation of AILA/IAAL, the editorial board of *AILA Review* has accepted to dedicate a volume to the problems around language choice for scientific communication. It is therefore with sincere pleasure that we, as guest editors, have collected a series of original contributions which draw a picture of actual and potential conflicts.

Possibly many AILA scholars and colleagues — especially the Anglophones (native speakers of English) or those professionally involved with the English language — have never felt that the exclusive use of this language in scientific communication could be a problem or be inequitable; on the contrary, the prevailing opinion seems to be that the present situation is absolutely natural or at least unavoidable. However, those who have been members of AILA since its foundation will remember that monolingualism was not its characteristic *ab initio*. Formerly, other languages of international use were also present, French *in primis*, as the acronym *AILA* itself testifies, which was only later extended to English *IAAL*. Some will also remember that, until the end of the Seventies of last century, a much higher degree of shared multilingualism was typical of academia, especially in international conferences, at least in the humanities. It was, in fact, only during the Eighties that a rapid and drastic change towards monolingualism took place, at first in the so-called *hard sciences* (natural sciences, medicine, technology, and mathematics) — under the threat of the 'bibliometric measurement' via the *impact factor* — and gradually also in the social sciences and the humanities.

It is for the first time, by this issue, that *AILA Review* tackles this development, with the strong support of a number of internationally known authors, who outline its scientific relevance and various options of language policy. In spite of the limited number of contributions that could be included for want of space, the volume displays views from diverse and not only Western parts of the world and different disciplines.

It begins with a paper by *Florian Coulmas* (*Deutsche Japanstudien* in Tokyo and *Universität Duisburg-Essen/* Germany) which presents the whole issue in the form of a Platonic dialogue, or rather of Marcus Aurelius' *Meditations*. It is a sagacious and amusing "colloquium of the author with himself" (the two characters are called by

AILA Review 20 (2007), 1–3. DOI 10.1075/aila.20.01amm
ISSN 1461–0213 / E-ISSN 1570–5595 © John Benjamins Publishing Company

the initial letters of his name and surname), which presents a wide range of social and personal conflicts around the issue and their implications.

It is followed by two papers focussing on the disadvantages of non-Anglophone scholars ensuing from the dominance of English in academic writing: the first one by *John Flowerdew* (then City University of Hong Kong, now University of Leeds) is a concise analysis of the concrete problems non-Anglophones are confronted with, under present conditions, in writing and publishing research articles. The enormous difficulties which academic prose poses for them are displayed through the case of a Chinese-English Hong Kong bilingual who, in spite of all his exposure to English, encounters enormous linguistic problems when trying to publish in this language. These problems are not so much rooted in lexis and phrasing but rather in discourse and cultural conventions which clash with the Anglophone gate-keepers' expectations who watch over largely non-written editorial rules and insist on adjusting to the style of *native speakers*.

The second of these contributions is the fruit of collective research of *Cristina Guardiano, M. Elena Favilla and Emilia Calaresu (Università di Modena e Reggio Emilia/* Italy) and links the problem of English as the sole language of international scientific communication to data from a recent survey on the language use of Italian-speaking academics and their perception of language choice for scientific publications.

Closely related to these results from Italy is the contribution by *Rainer Enrique Hamel (Universidad Autónoma Metropolitana de México/* Mexico), who outlines the recent history of language choice for international scientific communication and the predominance of English, focussing on periodicals, i.e. the most prestigious kind of scientific publications. The author's critical analysis highlights that the quality of scientific communication is nowadays to a large extent defined *a priori*, though not explicitly, by choice of language. In order to invert this tendency the author proposes various principles which he derives from scholars' critical self-observation of their language attitudes and behaviours. These principles, which could and should lead to researchers' re-orientation towards more plurilingualism, are listed in a sort of "pentalogue".

The disadvantages for non-Anglophones ensuing from the use of English as a kind of lingua franca are not only cultural-academic, but also economic. This aspect is dealt with, from two different perspectives, in the contributions by *Michele Gazzola* and *François Grin (Université de Genève/* Switzerland) and by *Philippe van Parijs (Université Catholique de Louvain/* Belgium). Their rigorous analyses lead to proposals for compensatory measures which aim at equalizing the linguistic costs for Anglophones and non-Anglophones. Not only do both diagnoses follow a similar path of analysis, but also they have related implications for possible interventions. Van Parijs' reasoning, in particular, implies that the adoption of a players' native language as a *lingua franca* unavoidably raises problems of linguistic justice. One of these problems is cooperative justice, i.e. the fair distribution of the costs of producing a public good which serves both sides. The article proposes a criterion for fair burden sharing and explores its policy implications. Gazzola and Grin, in contrast, assess the efficiency and fairness of alternative ways of managing multilingual communication in the case of linguistic diversity. Furthermore, their economic perspective should be helpful for assessing the pros and cons of different solutions and for arriving at principled and transparent decisions.

The multifaceted implications that language policy can have on its social context, are of central concern in the contribution by *Saran Kaur Gill* (Universiti Kebangsaa Malaysia), who highlights how recent developments in Malaysia (2003) are inter-twined with ideology, politics and especially language policy. In Malaysia, new regu-lations for each type and level of education, have substituted English for the official national language, Bahasa Malaysian, in science teaching. This decision has been mo-tivated by views of the country's need to improve competence in today's language of science. In a multilingual and multicultural country such as Malaysia, where various ethnic groups — like the Chinese and the Tamil, to name the numerically strongest — have got used to living together, such a language policy threatens to bring to an end the socio-political balance which finally has been achieved through mother-tongue edu-cation. A second potential downside of this policy — though perhaps not immediately obvious — could be the progressive loss of means of scientific conceptualization in the local languages, i.e. their loss of modernity or *Ausbau*.

The volume concludes with Ulrich Ammon's (*Universität Duisburg-Essen/* Ger-many) overview of — in his view — the reasonably safe knowledge about the topic, the remaining most urgent research questions, and the existing policy options including the proposal of firmly institutionalizing the topic in AILA in the form of a commit-tee entrusted with it. Ammon also requests more language norm tolerance vis-à-vis non-native speakers or their "right to linguistic peculiarity" and pictures the utopia of a future global language ("Globalish" or the like) derived but essentially different from English.

Since both guest editors share the same views the contributions to the present vol-ume were not always vetted by native speakers as long as verbal expressions appeared clear enough to the issue editors and acceptable to the reviewers.

The issue editors would like to thank the journal editor, Jasone Cenoz, and M. El-ena Favilla for their constant support and assistance, as well as the reviewers for their thoughtful comments and the authors for the kind and fruitful cooperation.

English monolingualism in scientific communication and progress in science, good or bad?

Florian Coulmas
Deutsches Institut für Japanstudien, Tokyo, Japan

I am not used to writing on assigned topics and do not intend to deviate from this principle in future, but since I am in various ways indebted to the editors of this special issue, I could not very well turn down their request to contribute to their endeavour. I have therefore consulted two experts in the field, F. and C., and asked them for their views on the question that makes up the title I was given. What follows is a précis of their discussion at which I was present. Since one of them objected to being taped, no recording of the discussion was made. However, both experts have authorized the text confirming that it is a fair rendition of their ideas and concerns.

C: Good morning, F, your forehead seems a bit clouded. What is it that worries you? Have a cup of tea.

F: Thank you and good morning to you, C, does it show, really? Well, the usual thing, I'm behind schedule. Silly me, I take deadlines at face value. The paper I promised for a special issue of the *International Journal of Stochastic Insignificance* (IJSI) is due tomorrow, and I just don't know how I can make it.

C: Too many committee meetings? Or are the results of the project you told me about the other day inconclusive? What is the problem?

F: No, it's not that, the tests are all very clear. I know exactly what I want to say, but I have to write it in English. You know, IJSI is the most important journal in the field, and they don't accept papers in other languages.

C: But what are you complaining about? Your English is better than mine, what's the big deal?!

F: You flatterer, that's hardly true. I can make myself understood, but that is not quite the same as writing fluently without inhibition and being certain that what the words mean is exactly what you want to say.

AILA Review 20 (2007), 5–13. DOI 10.1075/aila.20.03cou
ISSN 1461–0213 / E-ISSN 1570–5595 © John Benjamins Publishing Company

C: I cannot disagree with you here, but I believe this is a more general problem. Do you really want to go into it on this blissful morning? Some more tea?

F: No, um, I mean yes, thank you.

C: Well, whenever you write anything at all you cannot be completely sure that what you mean is what the text means, no matter in what language. Remember gavagai? If you have a fairly good command of the language, and a methodical mind and a disciplined way of setting pen to paper, there is no reason to believe that the discrepancy between what you mean and what you write is greater than a similar discrepancy in the text of a native speaker.

F: Sounds good, but the words just don't come to me so easily. I do notice a difference, you know. Sometimes I feel the language is ushering my thoughts ever so slightly in a certain direction rather than me being in charge marshalling the words to do what I want them to, pace Humpty Dumpty.

C: That surely is a sensation no monolingual can experience, not knowing an alternative. Monolinguals are much more at the mercy of their language than those of us who have more than one at our command. Also, monolinguals are seldom aware of the limitations of their vocabulary whereas we remark on a daily basis that a certain word doesn't match the concept we want to express or that a lexical differentiation in one language has no direct counterpart in another. You really shouldn't complain about having to write in a foreign language, it's an advantage. You are definitely more keenly aware of the problematic nature of language as a means that allows us to externalize our innermost thoughts, but only at the price of moulding them in a conventional form. Monolinguals often find it more difficult to understand that these forms are variable and that language and thought are two pairs of shoes.

F: Well, there you are right, thanks for the encouragement! You've always been good at looking at the bright side of things, but I'm in a fix. And I'm annoyed by the thought that my colleague in Oxbridge will have less trouble meeting the deadline, simply because English comes more naturally to her.

C: Gee, be a bit more charitable! Perhaps she finds it easier to write her paper, although that's by no means certain; but then your thoughts about stochastic processes as self-reproducing clusters of vacuous variables may benefit in unexpected ways from the extra mile you have to walk.

F: All right, all right, but mind you, if it is true as I think it is that a language is not quite the neutral instrument advocates of English monolingualism want us to believe then there is a real danger that the present predominance of English as the universal language of science will in the long run adversely affect the generation of knowledge.

C: That's a curious thing to say. For one thing, there are no advocates of English monolingualism. In the non-English-speaking world English is usually promoted as an auxiliary language only, a lingua franca that is in no way intended to replace other languages. And in the English-speaking world of which international conferences just happen to be a part, people go out of their way to avoid the appearance of arrogance and linguistic imperialism. The likes of Charles Wentworth Dilke have all but died out. He opined that people would be more truthful if only they spoke English (*Greater Britain: A Record of Travel in English-Speaking Countries*, London, 1868/69), but few people believe that nowadays. When the World Society for Anti-Ageing Research convenes in Acapulco, the organizers would even say "Buenos días, pardon my imperfect Spanish!". And so on.

F: You're right again, but intended or not, in practice, science functions ever more in a single language, and that can be harmful.

C: Why is that? What's the evidence?

F: Number one, there are things you can do in one language and not in another. That is incontrovertible, or is it not? Take WÚ or MU, the Chinese and Japanese words that mean 'nothing'.

C: That's straightforward enough. What can you say about nothing, anyway!

F: Hold on, you're blurring the issue. You will not understand the first thing about this word unless you study Buddhist philosophy first.

C: My, my! That's a pretty hefty claim to make, but with all due respect, I think there are some facts you have not considered. Of course you can talk about the niceties of nothing in English or any language, for that matter. The old Humboldtian — English speakers prefer to call it Whorfian — doctrine of linguistic determinism has little empirical evidence to back it up. No language is a prison house for thought. Languages are open systems that can be adapted to any purpose. Don't blame the language if it is its users who make things impenetrable. I am too much of a Cartesian to buy the idea that as a matter of principle you cannot express in one language what can be said in another. That an intellectual tradition developed in one language rather than another is a different matter. Are not the Greek tragedies meaningful in the garb of any language? Cannot kōans, the enigmatic stories Zen masters tell their disciples, be rendered into their languages? Or, if you prefer an example from science, did not a treatise with the sexy title *Zur Elektrodynamik bewegter Körper* revolutionize modern physics? It's not, as you may suspect, about group sex, but more widely known nowadays as the special theory of relativity. True, many physicists read German in 1905, but that is not my point. Clearly, the treatise lost nothing of its significance by being rendered from German into English and other languages. There is contents and there is form. Dualism is a powerful conceptual grid that helps you untangle the complex relationships between words and objects and concepts, although I have to admit it is in many ways premised on Western philosophy. Language as conceived in the Western tradition is built on dualism: a structure that relates contents and form.

F: I see what you are getting at. Language doesn't matter. But I do not concede yet. There are some other facts that speak against linguistic reductionism in science that you may want to take into account.

C: Who calls for linguistic reductionism?! But go on, please.

F: Thank you, very generous. Well, number two, important scientific insights tend to be ignored if published in a language other than English, and not just since yesterday. For example, the teachings of John Maynard Keynes were foreshadowed in the 1930s by the Copenhagen School of Economists and even put into practice in Sweden, but nobody noticed; for "great economic ideas were not expected to come from small countries" (John Kenneth Galbraith, *A History of Economics*, 1987, 225) or clad in small languages, I might add. Has anyone heard of a path breaking scientific discovery published in Portuguese or Bengali or Dutch of late? Is that because the Portuguese, Bengalis and Hollanders have nothing to say, or because Portuguese, Bengali and Dutch are unfit for scientific prose?

C: Surely not, but once again, you shouldn't confuse the languages with their speakers. The speakers have a choice, and if they have anything to say they are more likely than not to prefer to say it in English, because life is short, and because too much is being published anyway and if they want to get recognition for an original idea or discovery they had better publish it in English, and fast.

F: That isn't fair, is it?

C: Is history fair?

F: You mean to say, nothing can be done about it? That is succumbing not to reason but to power. If it were just the language it wouldn't be so bad, but the language comes with a lot of extra baggage. The majority of editors and board members of the most important international journals, such as IJSL, hail from Anglo-Saxon countries or were educated there. They are powerful gatekeepers. Unless you accept their ideas of how science ought to be done and its results presented you don't have a chance to get past them.

C: But chaos is a dangerous threat to the production of systematic and intersubjective knowledge. Isn't it a good thing that certain standards are enforced?

F: It stifles variety, imagination, creativity and innovation. The idea that there can be a single standard of optimizing scientific advancement is preposterous! There is such a thing as fashion and culture in science, you know, and of course vested interest. Why do you think huge amounts of money are allocated to research about the causes of obesity, or mini nukes, for that matter? The disinterested search for *episteme* is a dream long past nobody dreams anymore. 'Anything goes,' the apostles of postmodernity declared with much fanfare, but that is just the liberal smokescreen behind which a powerful monoculture evolved, a monoculture in science. The truth is — if you excuse the old-fashioned term — nothing goes unless you get funding and to get funding you have to publish in international journals, and to publish in international journals you've got to pen your stuff in English, and don't you dare to disregard the catechism!

C: Science is not religion.

F: Oh really, you don't say! In case you haven't noticed, quite a few scientists behave like ministrants. You have to go by the book. Abstract, Introduction, Methods, Results, Discussion, Conclusion, Acknowledgement, References, Amen. Don't deviate from the pattern if you want to get published, and don't use the word "which" because your editor has probably learnt that it has no place in a scientific paper. How tedious! Always the same pattern, the same style. Don't you tire of the ritual?

C: I read for content.

F: And you don't get upset about all these conformists who never ask what it is they are aping and who would never think of submitting a poem to a scholarly journal?

C: No, I can't get worked up about these trifles. Also, you might consider coming down from your high horse of the solitary intellectual truth-seeker in splendid isolation. Science is a social effort, and it is about being systematic and persistent. Common attitudes, common standards of behaviour, common questions and assumptions, and common forms are necessary. They change with time. We are all children of our time and more so than certain egomaniacs are happy to admit. Also, you could make your life easier by not taking these things too seriously. If you know the rules of the game you can play it. That's all. The formal requirements are just that, not a passport to a better understanding of the natural or the social world. In time they will change. Keep that in mind and you'll have more peace of mind.

F: You're a cynic.

C: I'd be miserable if I weren't, though I prefer 'sceptic'. I'm suspicious of apodictic statements. "This is how a scientific paper should be written". "English monolingualism in scientific communication is good". "English monolingualism in scientific communication is bad". Tertium non datur is not for me.

F: Hey, there's some common ground. It's better having a choice than not having a choice, right?

C: Agreed.

F: Well, there you are. We don't have a choice anymore!

C: True, my dear friend, but face it, 'freedom of choice' is rapidly degenerating into an advertising slogan compromised by genetic determinism, on one hand, and economic determinism, on the other.

F: Yeah, consumption is what counts. That holds for knowledge as for anything else. If you want to sell it you have to make sure that it appeals to the customer. Wrap it up in polished English and take it to the market. A piece of knowledge that comes with tildes, graves, let alone non-roman characters will find no buyers, right?

C: Calm down, please, and try to think of the advantages of having an international language of science. There are some, I assure you, and the downside may not be quite as dramatic as you seem to think. You mustn't look at a language as something that is forced down your throat. As soon as you are using it you contribute to it, and if it doesn't fit your needs, bend it in shape!

F: The editors won't allow it. You know that quite well.

C: Granted, they tend to be less tolerant with non-natives and writers who are perceived as such, but change, improvement, adjustment and augmentation are possible. Language is a collective product, not a natural species.

F: Sounds interesting, but I'm afraid I don't quite understand what you mean. Are you pointing the way to linguistic Darwinism, or are you arguing against it?

C: I certainly wouldn't call it Darwinism. Evolutionism is perhaps less tainted. Language *is* an adaptive instrument, and there is no reason to think its evolution has come to a conclusion, for language is also an artefact. You could look at the world's languages not as a set of different systems but as one system to which we have access through whatever words are uttered around us in our early years and to which we add continuously as we move along the path to eventual speechlessness. Individual languages which, linguists will tell you, are hard to distinguish one from another anyway, are largely a matter of historical and cultural evolution which means they are impermanent. The only value of each language's distinctness may be just that: not being the same as others. That's not much, is it? At the same time, with more than six and a half billion people babbling away continuously, the expressive potential of human language is being more fully utilized today than ever before, and English is leading the way. Its functional range is wider than that of most languages being as it is put to use for a greater variety of tasks and in more diverse parts of the world than any other language to date. English has proved to be quite flexible and adaptable incorporating a wealth of idioms from other tongues. For now it is the richest, most articulate and adaptable symbolic code humankind has developed. And as such English is a public good serviceable to humanity at large. It also has a sizeable speech community that is working at its improvement continuously. And you can be part of it.

F: By necessity rather than choice.

C: If you can't resist it you may as well embrace it. If you take consolation in philosophical sanction, thinkers from Epicurus to Marx have conceptualized freedom as insight into necessity.

F: The question then is just what necessity is dictated by, the mob?

C: You're not blunt, are you? If you are inclined to believe that nothing the crowd appreciates can be really tasteful and good, a position which in view of consumerism and mass culture seems eminently tenable, you may not want to buy my argument about language as a collective product and a public good that is being improved incessantly through use in speech and writing. But give it a chance, anyway.

F: I will, since I value your opinion. Yet, if English appears in such a rosy light as a public good, other languages have a similar claim, too. Today, quite a few languages that have been honed by many generations of their speakers to give expression to the finest conceptual distinctions in all specialized fields of knowledge are loosing out to English. They degenerate. The history of Arabic should be a lesson to all who care. In the Middle Ages it was the most highly cultivated language of the world second to none as a tool of science and poetry and philosophy. But today only few university courses in Arabic-speaking countries are taught in Arabic. Why is that so? Because scientists in these countries were trained in French and English, because no Arabic textbooks exist for all subjects, and because it is consequently hard to bring the terminology up-to-date.

C: Undeniably true what you're saying, but the fact is that scientists in these countries want to partake not just in the Arabic speaking scientific community but in that of the wider world which has become rather complex. There are not just different local, regional and national communities, but also, in certain fields at least, global communities that use English for its instrumental rather than symbolic value. "Legacy of Empire" and "propelled by military might", "unfair advantage", everything you're saying, yes, certainly. But nevertheless, the scientific community has made English its own.

F: Under these circumstances, bringing Arabic up-to-date for today's science is an uphill battle. The same holds for maintaining the expressive capacity of other languages that are used in science much less today than used to be the case. If present trends continue, the choice of English in science will before long no longer be a calculated preference but the default.

C: Yes, but luckily, there is translation. — I know what you want to say, *traduttore, traditore!* And, indeed, many are the hair-raising mistranslations. But in the end, you have to admit, it works if only you take the task seriously. Where would we be without translation?! When Europe was inundated by the Christian fanaticism of the Crusades, the philosophical work of pagan Aristotle was maintained in the world of Arabic learning. It was reintroduced to the Christian West through Arabic translations by the likes of Ibn Sina (Avicenna, 980–1037CE) who shared Aristotle's interest in medicine and Ibn Rushd (Avarroes, 1126–1198CE) who was the most famous Aristotelian scholar of his time. Translation is a productive process of interpretation. If today English is the chief source language of translation, and if more is translated out of English than into

English, that is perhaps a matter of regret for language nationalists. But for maintaining the registers of scientific discourse in these languages translating form English is most important all the same. In the globalising age translation is more important than ever.

F: Why do you think is that? Translation is just an additional burden and is moreover bound to be defective.

C: And if it is! Translation is also a test of meaningfulness. If what you want to say can be expressed in another language, and be it just approximately, you have one more proof that it isn't completely gormless, which is more than can be said of many scholarly papers that rightly nobody cares to translate. Plus, Scientese is a very strange code with many dialects that even native speakers of English have to learn deliberately. Scientific writing by both non-native and native speakers can be quite baffling because it is commonly bedevilled by awkward style, opaque jargon and sheer confusion. Think of making love and babies, for example.

> When an organism reproduces, replicas of its design features — its functional components — are introduced into its offspring. But the replication of the design of the parental machine is not always error-free. As a result, randomly modified designs (i.e., mutants) are introduced into populations of reproducers. Because living machines are already exactingly organized so that they cause the otherwise improbable outcome of constructing offspring machines, random modifications will usually introduce disruptions into the complex sequence of actions necessary for self-reproduction. Consequently, most newly modified but now defective designs will remove themselves from the population: a case of negative feedback (John Tooby, Leda Cosmides, "Evolutionary psychology: Conceptual foundations". In *Handbook of Evolutionary Psychology*, David M. Buss (ed.), Chichester: John Wiley&Sons Ltd., 2005).

Being a native speaker of English is hardly a sufficient condition for producing sentences like these. However, thanks to the creative efforts of several generations of scientists and other wordsmiths English has developed various specialized registers that make the negative feedback of living machines appear less surprising than it would be in many other languages. Of course, this wasn't always so. When English still had a long way to go to become the universal language of science, John Dryden, who did so much for uplifting it from a vulgar idiom to a respectable language of poetry, complained more than three hundred years ago:

> I am often put to a stand, in considering whether what I write be the idiom of the tongue, or false grammar, and nonsense couched beneath that specious name of Anglicism; and have no other way to clear my doubts, but by translating my English into Latin, and thereby trying what sense the words will bear in a more stable language (Dedication to *Troilus and Cressida*, 1679).

F: You're throwing this quote at me to let me see the advantages of translation?

C: Yes. And perhaps to offer some consolation.

F: English the latter-day Latin?

C: Historical parallels are deceptive, but, in a sense, yes. Latin used to be the yardstick. It came and went. In our day and age English is the yardstick. Was the predominance of Latin detrimental to the progress of science? It hardly makes sense to ask such a question. Only speculative answers could be put forth. What we know is that Latin was useful for some time and that the European "language makers" (Roy Harris) used it to transform vernaculars into veritable languages after its image. Translation was the proof of the pudding, for it is possible only between idioms that are equivalent in actual, rather than just potential, expressive power. To some extent the equivalence between what became the European national languages was assured by augmenting their lexicons with heaps of Latin words. Now English is both, the exemplar for translation and the donor and/or recycler of words. Obviously, there is no inherent need or guarantee that this role should forever be played by a European tongue.

F: Any thoughts about what might be the latter-day English?

C: Don't jump the gun! First, you have to acquiesce in the bilingualism that combines the local language with English as a supplementary universal written language. My guess is you and me we won't live to see it replaced by another pattern. Language legacies last long. But you know me as a cautious man. I don't make any predictions.

F: Thanks anyway. I am so glad you pointed that out to me. Now I am beginning to see the real significance of translation. Perhaps we should start studying Chinese and then translate what we write into that language to find out what sense the words will bear. What do you think? I have to run; or else I'll never keep my deadline. Thanks for the tea.

C: Thanks for keeping me company! See you around. Incidentally, I registered for an intensive Chinese course yesterday.

Author's address

Deutsches Institut fuer Japanstudien
Jochi Kioizaka Building 2F
7-1, Kioicho, Chiyoda-ku,
Tokyo 102-0094

http://www.dijtokyo.org
coulmas@dijtokyo.org

The non-Anglophone scholar on the periphery of scholarly publication

John Flowerdew
University of Leeds, UK

As a symptom of globalization and the marketization of the universities, more and more scholars, many or most, of whom use English as an additional language (EAL), are being required to published in English. This article presents some qualitative data which highlights some of the difficulties encountered by such writers. It first discusses a previously published case study of an EAL writer writing for publication, highlighting some of the difficulties encountered by this young scholar. It then goes on to consider a particular writing strategy adopted by some EAL writers which might be considered to be controversial, the copying of fragments of text from previously published work, and referred to here as language re-use. The final part of the paper discusses various approaches directed towards alleviating problems encountered by EAL writers such as those exemplified in the main body of the paper.

Introduction

With the pressures of globalization and the marketization of the academy (Aronowitz 2000; Giroux and Myrsiades 2001), more and more scholars need to write for international journals, which are invariably in English (e.g. Ammon 2001). Many, if not most, of these scholars do not have English as their mother tongue, but use English as an additional language. The difficulties encountered by such writers (henceforth EAL writers) in writing for publication are increasingly being documented (e.g. Ammon 2001; Burrough-Boenisch 2003; Casanave 2002; Flowerdew1999a, 1999b, 2000; Gosden 2003; Li 2002, 2005, 2006a, 2006b, 2007). Having learned the language in the formal setting of the school and/or university rather than being brought up with it in the home, the challenge for most EAL writers to write at an appropriate level for publication in international journals is considerable. EAL writers are clearly, therefore, at a disadvantage compared to their native speaker peers (Ammon 2001; Flowerdew in press; van Dijk 1994). In order to achieve an acceptable level of performance, EAL writers may need to spend time and money in improving their English and they will

AILA Review 20 (2007), 14–27. DOI 10.1075/aila.20.04flo
ISSN 1461–0213 / E-ISSN 1570–5595 © John Benjamins Publishing Company

probably need to spend more time than their L1 counterparts in doing the necessary reading and actual writing that is required for the production of a research article. They will also probably need to spend more time dealing with editors' and reviewers' comments. In addition, as well as writing for publication in English, they may still need to develop the necessary skills for writing in their first language (Curry and Lillis 2004).

In this article I would like to provide some qualitative data which further highlights the difficulties of EAL writers. I will first discuss a case study of an EAL writer writing for publication in Hong Kong (Flowerdew 2000). I will then talk about language re-use, or the copying of fragments of text, a particular writing strategy adopted by some Mainland Chinese EAL writers and which might be considered to be controversial (Flowerdew and Li 2007). In my discussion section, I will consider various approaches directed towards alleviating problems encountered by EAL writers such as those exemplified in the main body of the paper.

A case study of a Hong Kong EAL writer writing for publication

In the late nineties I conducted a study of Hong Kong Cantonese L1 academics (across the disciplines) and their publishing practices (Flowerdew 1999a, 1999b, 1999c, 2000, 2001, 2005). As part of this project I published a case study of the attempts of a young Hong Kong scholar in mass communication to publish a paper in an international refereed journal. The participant, pseudonym Oliver, recently returned from doctoral study in the United States, was working as an assistant professor in a Hong Kong university and was under a lot of pressure to obtain publications in support of his impending contract renewal. In Hong Kong career decisions are very much dependent upon publication in international refereed journal articles. As Oliver stated, it was extremely important for him to publish in English-medium journals, because all of the important journals in his field are in that language and there are no equivalent Chinese journals.

Oliver had Cantonese as his mother tongue, but his background in English was very considerable. His first contact with English was in kindergarten. He had attended English-medium elementary and secondary schools, his undergraduate study was at a bilingual Hong Kong university, and he had conducted his MA and PhD study in the United States. Oliver was ambiguous about whether he considered Chinese or English as his mother tongue, but as far as academic writing was concerned English was his preferred language, because that had been the language he had primarily used throughout his study. In spite of all of this exposure to English, as the case study demonstrates, Oliver still had problems with publishing in English.

One important problem in publishing, as far as Oliver was concerned, was prejudice against EAL writers. As he stated:

> I think Hong Kong scholars to be published in international journals is real hard. I
> think first of all it's the language problem. I think the journal editors' first impression

of your manuscript they discover that it is not written by a native-speaker — no matter how brilliant your idea they will have the tendency to reject.

Oliver resented the labelling effect of being classed as a "non-native speaker" by journal reviewers:

What makes me feel bad is I get letters from the reviewer and in the first two sentences it will say this is definitely not written by a native speaker — they shouldn't point this out as part of the main criteria for rejecting the article.

In addition to the language problem per se Oliver was also conscious of another difficulty of relevance for EAL writers (albeit less directly so), the difficulty of being on the "periphery" and out of the mainstream. Oliver felt that he was not able to be up to date with what was going on in his discipline because of his relative isolation from scholars in the United States. He stated that when he was in the United States he was able to consult freely with his mentors, to attend many conferences, and to get on a plane and go to another city to discuss with colleagues if he had a problem with a paper. Although this situation is primarily a logistical one, it is also relevant to language, because the opportunities Oliver was missing would have involved discussion in English and even the receipt of advice on his use of language. By not participating in these encounters, Oliver was losing his facility in using the particular type of English used in the target register of his discipline.

With regard to the specific article that was the focus of the case study in question, Oliver spent about 18 months working on the manuscript and its various revisions. The first submission was a rejection and the response to the second one was that the article could not be published in time for Oliver's contract renewal. With the third submission the editors expressed some interest and said the paper could be publishable with very considerable revision. In spite of expressing interest in the article, the editor rather enigmatically suggested that Oliver might like to consider other journals. Nevertheless, Oliver decided to persevere with this journal. There followed some eight months of negotiation and revision.

Oliver employed the services of a local L1 English speaker to help him with editing and revising. The L1 editor did not find the work he was asked to do entirely satisfactory. From his point of view Oliver did not give him enough consultation on what was required and how the editing was being carried out. It seemed that Oliver expected the L1 editor to be able to "fix up" the article without any need for interaction with him, while the L1 editor felt that his knowledge of the discipline was inadequate for him to revise the paper without the assistance of the author.

Following resubmission, nevertheless, Oliver was told that his paper was provisionally accepted, but on condition that he was able "to undertake the editing or arrange for the editing to be done by someone else following the examples presented to you." (The letter was accompanied by several pages of the manuscript which had been heavily edited both in terms of language and organization by an assistant editor.)

In addition, the editor again suggested that Oliver might like to submit his article to another journal, one which might have better facilities for doing the editing work required of Oliver's manuscript.

Oliver again decided to persevere and further editing was done by the local L1 editor, who was again dissatisfied with the minimal direction given to him by Oliver. In the following months there was further correspondence and revision, with the assistant editor of the journal making an extreme number of changes, including changing the language of nearly every sentence. The reaction of the L1 editor was as follows:

> In the end, I have to believe that for the author the entire process must have been extremely stressful. Finding a suitable L1 editor, dealing with the subsequent edits and contending with the vagaries regarding content, as well as having to address the editorial demands of the journal editor and the reviewers all represent L2 challenges which seem far beyond those experienced by L1 scholars.

As for Oliver, he was, of course, delighted to finally achieve publication. In addition, he learned from the experience that he needed to spend more time considering the rhetorical dimension of his writing. He had spent too much time focussing on the content and relied too much on the L1 editor to address rhetorical problems in his paper, stating that "when I write another article — the current article I am writing — I will be more focussed and more concentrated on the style rather than a lot of the content and stuff like that."

To sum up, although many of the problems encountered by Oliver might have been shared by an L1 writer, his problems as an EAL writer meant that he had to spend more time in writing the paper and revising it than an L1 writer would have had to do. In addition, due to his geographical situation on the periphery, he was denied the many advantages of being in the centre, including the possibility of networking with native speakers and developing and maintaining his competence in the particular type of English required by the register of his discipline.

Copying practices of doctoral science students in Mainland China

Having documented the publication efforts of one EAL writer based in Hong Kong, I will now turn to another group of writers, doctoral research students in one university in Mainland China. Before discussing the writing practices of these writers, I would like to contextualise this discussion by reporting on a newspaper story to do with plagiarism. The story appeared in the *Wall Street Journal* of August 16, 2006 as a two page spread under large headlines, as follows:

Familiar words: plagiarism stirs controversy at Ohio University

The article describes how the son of a surgeon from Columbus, Ohio, Thoma Matrka, was enrolled in a master's degree in mechanical engineering at Ohio State University and that he had difficulty in getting his thesis proposal approved. As a result he started going to the library to find inspiration in previously completed theses. He discovered that one thesis, by a student from Thailand, contained evidence of plagiarism. The example is given of the almost direct copying of the opening sentence from another thesis.

> Original text:
> "Quenching is a thermal treatment process for metal alloys that must be controlled to ensure the formation of desirable transformation products."

> Plagiarised text:
> "Quenching — a thermal treatment process for metal alloys — must be controlled for the formation of desirable transformation products."

Mr. Matrka also found dozens of additional pages of copied material, in addition to pages of equations and language from another thesis. Although these sources were cited in the bibliography, there was no in-text indication that the copied material had been taken from another source. Later Mr. Matrka went on to investigate further and discovered 29 plagiarised theses. Although it is not stated in the article if the plagiarised theses were written by EAL writers, the first example is clearly identified as a student from Thailand. The fact that the journalist does not mention where the writers of the other theses were from, along with the nature of the example provided, suggests that they were also EAL writers.

So in this article we have the story of an L1 writer who is resentful of the copying practices of fellow students (including at least one, if not all, EAL writers). It is notable however, that the reason given for Mr. Matrka's "frustration" was that classmates such as these were getting their proposals approved, while he was being unsuccessful in this regard (although he later succeeded).

I will return to this case later. First, I would like to look at the issue of copying from a different perspective, that of EAL writers. I will base my discussion on a project I have conducted with a Chinese colleague, Yongyan Li (Flowerdew and Li 2007). In this project a group of doctoral research students were interviewed about their copying practices and their writing was analysed to identify examples of copying. This group of EAL writers had a totally different view about copying the work of others to that of Mr. Matrka as described above. These young scholars were under heavy pressure to publish in indexed journals, as it was a graduation requirement. The writing practices of this group of EAL writers involved using on-line published articles related to their research topic as a source for copying-and-pasting set phrases. To give an example, the following is a stretch of text, as handed in to a supervisor by one of these researchers:

> *Student text*
> Formation of oxynitride alloys and the Burstein-Moss effect with high charge carrier concentrations may be responsible for sizable changes in the bandgap. [6] … … [7]. J. Wu et al. persisted that the electron concentration dependence of

the optical absorption edge energy was <u>fully accounted for by the Burstein–Moss</u> <u>shift</u>, <u>O and H impurities</u> couldn't <u>fully account for the free electron concentration</u> <u>in the films.</u> [8]

In this extract, the numbers in square brackets are citations to the texts which the student has re-used. If we search these cited texts we can identify certain phrases which have been re-used in the student text. In the following extract, for example, we find pieces of text which were re-used in the first two lines of the student text (underlining indicates copied text) (notice that the student, although not acknowledging that this is an exact citation, nevertheless indicates the source, with the footnote in square brackets [6]):

> *Source text [6]: (in a review article)*
> <u>The Burstein-Moss effect</u> in polycrystalline samples<u> with high charge carrier</u> <u>concentrations may</u> also <u>be responsible for sizable changes in the band gap</u>.

The next extract is from another source text and contains phrases which can be matched with their counterparts in the student text cited above (lines 3–5) (notice again how the student text acknowledges the source with the footnote in square brackets [8]):

> *Source text [8]: (in the Abstract of a research article)*
> <u>The electron concentration dependence of the optical absorption edge energy</u> is <u>fully accounted for by the Burstein–Moss shift</u>. Results of secondary ion mass spectrometry measurements indicate that <u>O and H impurities</u> cannot <u>fully ac-</u> <u>count for the free electron concentration in the films.</u>

This example and others provided by Flowerdew and Li (2007), which they refer to as "language re-use", bear a remarkable similarity to the type of copying cited above in the case of the Thai student so resented by Mr. Matrka. It is notable also that the Thai student, like the Chinese students, included citations where copying was carried out.

Now, I mentioned before how the Chinese EAL writers in this study had a very different view of copying practices such as these as did the L1 writer, Mr. Matrka.

To begin with, they were quite open about what they were doing and assisted the researchers in tracing copied material from source texts and explaining their practices. There follows a series of quotations from interviews with the EAL writers. It is clear from these quotations that these writers felt fully justified in their copying practices, although they had different justifications according to the different sections of the research article. Thus copying in the introduction was justified by one writer as follows:

> As long as you give the source — showing it's not your work — it's OK even if you copy a paragraph[1] — sometimes you modify more, other times less — depending on your circumstances. The key is you give the source and show it's others' work or results, not yours.

In the methods section the following justification was given. Here the copying is in fact from a paper published by a co-worker:

> Our lab has this set of established, successful experimental methods, he [the lab-
> mate] wrote it into his paper; when I arrived, the lab taught me this set of meth-
> ods, then I did my experiments. But he has expressed it into words, so when I
> wrote mine, I referred to his words, with some modification according to my ex-
> periments. Even if I hadn't used his words, we have generally the same methods.

For the results section, often figures need to be referred to. The following is the justification for copying given by one of the writers for interpreting a figure:

> It's mainly according to content. Things like this, the content is similar, adopt it, no
> problem, and I won't make a mistake.

As I said, these writers do not feel they are doing anything wrong with these practices.
They adopt these copying practices because they do not have the confidence in their
own English to express what they need to say appropriately. This position is neatly
summed up in the previous quotation: "adopt it, no problem, and I won't make a mistake". So there is an element of fear which is motivating these young EAL writers to
write as they do.

The justifications of these writers are based on two facts. First, they are not taking
the ideas of other writers, only the language which is chosen by those more proficient
writers to convey what is already established knowledge. Second, they provide references to the articles which they have drawn upon, thus acknowledging that they have
referred to these other writers.

So are these writers justified in their justifications? I am not ready to unequivocally pass judgment one way or the other. But it is worth pointing out that all of this
can be related to theories of intertextuality and Kristeva's idea of a text as "a mosaic of
quotations" and of one text as "the absorption and transformation of another" (Kristeva 1980:66). If one adopts Kristeva's theory then this puts a whole different perspective
on plagiarism as it is conceived of in the *Wall Street Journal* article and tends to support
what the Chinese writers are doing.[2]

This type of writing, in fact is not much different to recent innovative uses of spe-
cialist corpora in the teaching of academic writing. Cargill and O'Connor (2006: 210)
talk about "the concept of constructing a corpus of articles from their [EAL writers']
own discipline to use as a source of data for ongoing language learning." They also talk
about using what they refer to as "sentence templates", i.e. "sentence structures that
could usefully be re-used with different noun phrases inserted." Lee and Swales (2006)
refer to this form of writing instruction as "corpus-informed EAP". Already in 1993, I
myself (Flowerdew 1993) was advocating this form of writing apprenticeship.

Also, it is worth bearing in mind that this has been made possible largely with the
use of word processors as a basic tool of writing and with access to on-line source texts.
These two phenomena have made writing a whole different activity to what it was in
the past. Perhaps we need also to review our notions of plagiarism.

To draw some conclusions from this case of the Chinese doctoral students, we have seen that they are driven to the particular writing strategy of copy-and-paste, which some might call plagiarism, because of their limited competence and lack of confidence in their English and the very high stakes "game" they find themselves in of having to publish in journals published in English to graduate. These EAL writers are driven by fear of making inappropriate choices if they use "their own" language. While some of the difficulties noted in the first of the cases presented in this paper, that of the Hong Kong EAL writer, Oliver, might be shared by L1 writers (questions of organization etc.), in this second case, the problems encountered by the Mainland Chinese doctoral science students seem to be more clearly EAL problems. Although L1 writers may use copy-and-paste in some cases (research needs to be done on this), they are highly unlikely to need to do it to anything near like the extent of the Chinese writers.

Although the two cases presented here are strikingly different, they do have a lot in common. Both the Hong Kong writer and the Mainland Chinese writers find themselves on the periphery. They do not have access to the mainstream, where they might find support from their L1 peers. The case is more serious for the Mainland scholars, because they do not have access to L1 editors. The Hong Kong Chinese writer, Oliver, in this respect is more fortunate in being able to draw upon the services of an L1 editor (although, as we have seen, because he is not an expert in the field, the amount of assistance this editor is able to give is limited). It seems there are degrees of "peripherality".

Discussion

I began this article by noting the increasing need of scholars to publish internationally in English and that many, if not most, of these scholars were EAL writers. I then considered a case study of one EAL writer in Hong Kong and his efforts in getting a paper published This was followed by a consideration of the notion of plagiarism and language re-use, first from the perspective of an L1 writer in the United States and then through the lens of a group of EAL writers in Mainland China. I think that in the data that I have presented and the way that I have presented it demonstrates that I sympathize very much with the plight of the EAL writer.

In this discussion I would like to consider some of the broader implications of what I have presented here. It is clear that EAL scholars may have great difficulty in achieving publication because of language difficulties. I am not saying that L1 writers do not also have difficulties. Lillis (cited in Harwood and Hadley 2004: 355) describes academic writing as 'mysterious', and rightly, in my view, states that its practices are poorly understood not only by students but also by teachers. This impenetrability of academic writing is likely shared among both L1 and EAL writers. However, I would not go as far as Swales (2004: 52), who has written that "[t]he difficulties typically experienced by NNS academics in writing English are (certain mechanics such as article usage aside) au fond pretty similar to those typically experienced by native speakers." I would like to think that the data I have presented in this paper is evidence that this is not the case, at least for the writers reported upon here.[3]

What positions might be adopted by scholars and practitioners directed towards alleviating the plight of the EAL writer and establishing a more equitable situation? I think there are a number of alternatives, all of which have parallels in the English for Academic Purposes literature.[4] In this literature three positions vis a vis the teaching of English for Academic Purposes are posited. First, there is the "pragmatic" perspective, which argues that learners should be helped to comply as best they can with the conventions of the academy (Allison 1996; Swales 1990). Second, there is the "critical" perspective, which encourages a questioning of the status quo and demands changes to educational practices to make these practices more inclusive of learners from second language backgrounds (Benesch 1993, 2001; Pennycook 1997). Third, there is a middle way, what Harwood and Hadley (2004) refer to as the "critical pragmatic" view (Benesch 2001; Pennycook 1994), which argues for helping learners to achieve the necessary goals, on the one hand, but on the other hand, encouraging them to develop a questioning attitude towards what is being demanded of them.[5]

Now it would seem that these approaches might well be applied to the question of scholarly publishing. The pragmatic approach would be to encourage a focus on helping EAL writers approximate as closely as they can to L1 norms. This would mean encouraging greater provision of academic writing programmes and support facilities (Benfield and Feak 2006; Cargill and O'Connor 2006; Curry and Lillis 2004; Lillis and Curry 2006). Such provision might draw on a range of scholarly and applied work: discourse and genre analysis of academic articles (e.g. Swales, 1990, 2004; work published in journals such as *English for Specific Purposes* and *Journal of English for Academic Purposes*); case studies of successful (and not so successful) EAL writers (Belcher and Connor 2001; Curry and Lillis 2004; Flowerdew 2000; Gosden 1995; Li 2007; Lillis and Curry 2006); learning materials for scholarly writing (Swales and Feak 1994, 2000; Weissberg and Buker 1990); advice on how to negotiate with editors and reviewers (Mišak, Marušić and Marušić 2005, Li and Flowerdew 2007), and the provision of editing and translation services (Burrough-Boenisch 2003; Kerans 2001; Könner 1994; Ventola and Mauranen 1991).

The critical approach, on the other hand, would be to demand more equality of opportunity for EAL writers, by, for example, alerting EAL writers to the difficulties and disadvantage of their community (Ammon 2001; Flowerdew in press; Hayter 2004; Kirkman 1996) and the overall hegemony of English (Canagarajah 2002a; Swales 1997), encouraging greater value to be placed on publication in local languages (Ammon 2001; Salager-Meyer 2007; Ehlich 2005), encouraging editors to be more accepting of non-standard English (Ammon 2000; Belcher in press; Berns 2005; Canagarajah 2002b; Kachru 1995; Seidlhofer 2001; Yakhontova 2001), encouraging EAL writers to be more assertive in their dealings with editors and reviewers (Belcher in press; Burrough-Boenisch 2003; Casanave 2002; Gosden 2003; Li 2006a; Ramanathan 2002), and educating editors in how to deal supportively with EAL writers (Belcher in press; Canagarajah 2002b; Flowerdew 2001; McKay 2003).

The critical pragmatic approach, the middle way, would encourage training for EAL writers, on the one hand, but on the other, emphasise that there are alternatives available to them and that EAL writers should be made aware of these options. This approach, while encouraging a critical mind-set would at the same time alert EAL writers to the possible repercussions of some of the critical actions. For example, publication in local languages might be detrimental to career development, insistence on the validity of certain language re-use practices might give rise to accusations of plagiarism, insistence on writing in non-standard English might lead to rejection by editors and reviewers.

I should perhaps make my own position clear on this. Researchers in the area of EAL publishing, it seems to me, are in a double bind. On the one hand, their conscience tells them to promote the critical approach and contest the iniquities of the status quo. Reality, on the other hand, tells them that to do so may be at the expense of individual EAL scholars. As already mentioned, to argue for publication in a local language, for example, an argument which ideologically carries great weight, may lead to negative repercussions on the career prospects of EAL writers if they follow this course of action.

It seems to me that it may be helpful in resolving this dilemma if a distinction is made between scholarly- and practitioner-oriented work. As far as the former is concerned, applied linguistics scholarship such as that cited in this paper can play an important role in educating editors, reviewers and academe at large to the negative aspects of the status quo and arguing for reform. A critical approach would seem to be appropriate, therefore, as far as our scholarly endeavours are concerned. Regarding the practitioner-oriented work, on the other hand, here care needs to be taken not to jeopardise the career prospects of our target community of EAL scholars. Given the dangers of the possible negative repercussions of the critical approach, the critical pragmatic approach would seem to be the more valid one for our practitioners.

Within the critical-pragmatism paradigm, however, sensitivity needs to be applied according to different contexts. In some contexts, for example, where there are plentiful financial resources, the establishment of editorial support services can be argued for, but where financial resources are lacking, then this may be an unrealistic goal. In some institutions great emphasis may be put on publication in citation-indexed journals and career decisions may be made on the basis of output in such journals. Encouraging practitioners to publish in non-English, non-indexed journals in such situations might then not be a good option.

Whichever approach is adopted, one thing is clear, and that is that the difficulties encountered by EAL writers, as documented in the literature and as is clear from the two cases presented in this paper, are immense. There therefore remains a tremendous amount of work to be done. On the one hand, there needs to be a focus on educating EAL scholars, L1 scholars, academe in general, and the world at large about the difficulties experienced by EAL scholars and their ramifications. On the other hand, strategies need to be developed for helping EAL scholars to overcome these difficulties.

Notes

1. It should be noted that there were in fact no examples in this EAL writer's manuscripts of the copying of whole paragraphs. The copying was limited to the level of the phrase, as exemplified in the other examples provided in this paper.

2. See e.g., Canagarajah (2002a), Hu (2001), Pennycook (1996), and Scollon (1995) for arguments for a consideration of plagiarism relative to particular cultural, disciplinary, and rhetorical contexts.

3. Some of the data presented in this paper, along with some other related material, was presented at an international conference ("Publishing and Presenting Research Internationally: Issues for speakers of English as an Additional Language", University of La Laguna, Tenerife, Spain, January 11–13, 2007). In the closing session of the conference Swales in fact stated that his claim had perhaps been too strong.

4. By English for Academic Purposes I am referring to the whole enterprise of preparing learners to study in English, of which publication is only one aspect.

5. This position was in fact already argued for in 1994 by Pennycook (1994:317).

References

Aronowitz, S. 2000. *The Knowledge Factory: Dismantling the corporate university and creating true higher learning.* Boston MA: Beacon Press.

Allison, D. 1996. Pragmatist discourse and English for Academic Purposes. *English for Specific Purposes* 15: 85–103.

Ammon, U. 2000. Towards more fairness in international English: Linguistic rights of non-native speakers? In *Rights to Language: Equity, power and education,* R. Phillipson (ed.), 111–116. Mahwah NJ: Lawrence Erlbaum Associates.

Ammon, U. 2001. *The Dominance of English as a Language of Science: Effects on other languages and language communities.* Berlin: Mouton de Gruyter.

Belcher, D. In press. Seeking acceptance in an English-only research world. *Journal of Second Language Writing.*

Belcher, D. & Connor, U. 2001. *Reflections on Multiliterate Lives.* Clevedon: Multilingual Matters.

Benesch, S. 1993. ESL, ideology, and the politics of pragmatism. *TESOL Quarterly* 27: 705–717.

Benesch, S. 2001. *Critical English for Academic Purposes: Theory, politics, and practice.* Mahwah NJ: Lawrence Erlbaum Associates.

Benfield, J. R. & Feak, C. B. 2006. How authors can cope with the burden of English as an international language. *Chest* 129: 11728–11729.

Berns, M. 2005. Expanding on the expanding circle: Where do WE go from here? *World Englishes* 24: 85–93.

Burrough-Boenisch, J. 2003. Shapers of published NNS research articles. *Journal of Second Language Writing* 12: 223–243.

Canagarajah, A.S. 2002a. *Critical Academic Writing and Multilingual Students.* Ann
Arbor MI: University of Michigan Press.

Canagarajah, A.S. 2002b. *A Geopolitics of Academic Writing.* Pittsburgh PA: University of Pittsburgh Press.

Cargill, M. & O'Connor, P. 2006. Developing Chinese scientists' skills for publishing in English: Evaluating collaborating-colleague workshops based on genre analysis. *Journal of English for Academic Purposes* 5: 207–221.

Casanave, C.P. 2002. *Writing Games: Multicultural case studies of academic literacy practices in higher education.* Mahwah NJ: Lawrence Erlbaum Associates.

Curry, M. J. & Lillis, T. 2004. Multilingual scholars and the imperative to publish in English: Negotiating interests, demands, and rewards. *TESOL Quarterly* 38: 663–688.

Ehlich, K. 2005. Plurilingualism in scientific communication — illusion or necessity? Paper presented at International Languages for Specific Purposes Conference, University of Bergamo, Italy, August 2005.

Flowerdew, J. 1993. A process, or educational, approach to the teaching of professional genres. *ELT Journal* 47: 305–316.

Flowerdew, J. 1999a. Writing for scholarly publication in English: The case of Hong Kong. *Journal of Second Language Writing* 8: 123–145.

Flowerdew, J. 1999b. Problems in writing for scholarly publication in English: The case of Hong Kong. *Journal of Second Language Writing* 8: 243–264.

Flowerdew, J. 1999c. An interview with Sandra McKay, Editor of TESOL Quarterly. *Asian Journal of English Language Teaching* 9: 99–103.

Flowerdew, J. 2000. Discourse community, legitimate peripheral participation, and the nonnative-English-speaking scholar. *TESOL Quarterly* 34: 127–150.

Flowerdew, J. 2001. Attitudes of journal editors to non-native-speaker contributions: An interview study. *TESOL Quarterly* 35: 121–150.

Flowerdew, J. 2005. A multi-method approach to research into processes of scholarly writing for publication. In *Second Language Writing research: Perspectives on the process of knowledge construction*, P. Kei Matsuda & T. Silva (eds.), 65–77. Mahwah NJ: Lawrence Erlbaum Associates.

Flowerdew, J. In press. Scholarly writers who use English as an Additional Language: What can Goffman's *Stigma* tell us? *Journal of English for Academic Purposes.*

Flowerdew, J. & Li, Y.-Y. (2007). Language re-use among Chinese apprentice scientists writing for publication. *Applied Linguistics* 28: 440–465.

Giroux, H. A. & Myrsiades, K. (eds.). 2001. *Beyond the Corporate University: Culture and pedagogy in the new millennium.* Lanham MD: Rowman and Littlefield.

Gosden, H. 1995. Success in research article writing and revision: A social constructionist perspective. *English for Specific Purpose* 14: 35–57.

Gosden, H. 2003. *Why not give us the full story?* Functions of referees' comments in peer reviews of scientific research papers. *Journal of English for Academic Purposes* 2(2): 87–101.

Harwood N. & Hadley, G. 2004. Demystifying institutional practices: Critical pragmatism and the teaching of academic writing. *English for Specific Purposes* 23: 355–377.

Hayter, J. P. 1994. English is a barrier. *British Medical Journal* 309: 666.

Hu, J. M. 2001. The Academic Writing of Chinese Graduate Students in Science and Engineering: Processes and challenges. PhD dissertation, University of British Columbia, Vancouver.

Kachru, Y. 1995. Contrastive rhetoric in world English. *English Today* 41: 21–31.

Kerans, M. E. 2001. Eliciting substantive revision of manuscripts for peer review through process-oriented conferences with Spanish scientists. In *Trabajos en linguistica aplicada*, C. Muñoz (ed.), 339–347. Barcelona: Universitat de Barcelona.

Kirkman, J. 1996. Confine yourself to forms of English that are easily understood. *British Medical Journal* 313: 1321–1322.

Kristeva, J. 1980. *Desire in Language: A semiotic approach to literature and art.* New York NY: Columbia University Press.

Könner, A. 1994. Bioscript — an editorial service for scientists. *English Today* 10: 4–48.

Lee, D. & Swales, J. 2006. A corpus-based EAP course for NNS doctoral students: Moving from available specialized corpora to self-compiled corpora. *English for Specific Purposes*, 25: 56–75.

Li, Y.-Y. 2002. Writing for international publication: The perception of Chinese doctoral researchers. *Asian Journal of English Language Teaching* 12: 179–193.

Li, Y.-Y. 2005. Multidimensional enculturation: The case of an EFL Chinese doctoral student. *Journal of Asian Pacific Communication* 15: 153–170.

Li, Y.-Y. 2006a. Negotiating knowledge contribution to multiple discourse communities: A doctoral student of computer science writing for publication. *Journal of Second Language Writing* 15: 159–178.

Li, Y.-Y. 2006b. A doctoral student of physics writing for international publication: A sociopolitically-oriented case study. *English for Specific Purposes* 25: 456–478.

Li, Y.-Y. 2007. Apprentice scholarly writing in a *community of practice*: An intraview of an NNES graduate student writing a research article. *TESOL Quarterly* 41: 55–79.

Li, Y.-Y. & Flowerdew, J. 2007. Shaping Chinese novice scientists' manuscripts for publication. *Journal of Second Language Writing* 16: 100–117 .

Lillis, T. & Curry, M.J. 2006. Professional academic writing by multilingual scholars: Interactions with literacy brokers in the production of English-medium texts, *Written Communication* 23: 3–35.

McKay, S.L. 2003. Reflections on being a gatekeeper. In *Writing for Scholarly Publication: Behind the scenes in language education*, C.P. Casanave & S. Vandrick (eds.), 91–102. Mahwah NJ.: Lawrence Erlbaum Associates.

Mišak, A. Marušić M. & Marušić A. 2005. Manuscript editing as a way of teaching academic writing: Experience from a small scientific journal. *Journal of Second Language Writing* 14: 122–131.

Pennycook, A. 1994. *The Cultural Politics of English as an International Language.* London: Longman.

Pennycook, A. 1996. Borrowing others' words: Text, ownership, memory, and plagiarism. *TESOL Quarterly* 30: 201–230.

Pennycook, A. 1997. Vulgar pragmatism, critical pragmatism, and EAP. *English for Specific Purposes* 16: 253–269.

Ramanathan, V. 2002. *The Politics of TESOL Education.* London: Routledge.

Salager-Meyer, F. 2007. Publishing internationally in peripheral (a.k.a. developing) countries: Challenges for the future. Paper presented at international conference on publishing and presenting research internationally: Issues for speakers of English as an Additional Language. University of La Laguna, Tenerife, Spain.

Scollon, R. 1995. Plagiarism and ideology: Identity in intercultural discourse. *Language in Society* 24: 1–28.

Seidlhofer, B. 2001. Closing a conceptual gap: The case for a description of English as a lingua franca. *International Journal of Applied Linguistics* 11: 133–158.

Swales, M.J. 1990. *Genre Analysis: English in academic and research settings.* Cambridge: CUP.

Swales, J. 1997. English as Tyrannosaurus Rex. *World Englishes* 16: 373–382.

Swales, J. M. 2004. *Research Genres.* Cambridge: CUP.

Swales, J. M. & Feak, C. B. 1994. *Academic Writing for Graduate Students.* Ann Arbor MI: University of Michigan Press.

Swales, J. M. & Feak, C. B. 2000. *English in Today's Research World: A guide for writers.* Ann Arbor MI: University of Michigan Press.

Yakhontova, T. 2001. *Selling* or *Telling?* The issue of cultural variation in research genres. In *Academic Discourse*, J. Flowerdew (ed.), 216–232. London: Longman.

Van Dijk, T. A. 1994. Academic Nationalism. Editorial. *Discourse and Society* 5(3): 275–276.

Ventola, E. & Mauranen, A. 1991. Non-native writing and native revising of scientific articles. In *Functional and Systemic Linguistics: Approaches and uses,* E. Ventola (ed.), 457–492. Berlin: Mouton de Gruyter.

Weissberg, R. & Buker, S. 1990. *Writing up Research: Experimental research report writing for students of English.* Englewood Cliffs NJ: Prentice Hall Regents.

Author's address

Dr John Flowerdew
Professor of Applied Linguistics
Centre for Language Education Research
School of Education
University of Leeds
Leeds LS2 9JT
UK

john.flowerdew@education.leeds.ac.uk

Stereotypes about English as the language of science*

Cristina Guardiano, M. Elena Favilla and Emilia Calaresu
Università di Modena-Reggio Emilia, Italy

The progressive spread of English as the main language of international scientific communication has been interpreted in many different ways by several scholars. The paper presents a brief review of the scientific debate on such topics, focusing on the main stereotypes which have been created in order to provide explanations for the development of English as the language of science, and on the perception of non-Anglophone scholars on the reasons of the predominance of English in scientific literature and their disadvantages with respect to native speakers.

Frequently used stereotypes on English as the language of science are analyzed and discussed in reference to the motivations asserted by linguists and non-linguists. A double ideological evidence can be registered: (1) arguments essentially consist in *a-posteriori* justifications, (2) English — far away from representing a free choice for non-native scholars — is perceived as the repository of the linguistic power that is desired and worshipped.

The overview closes with the results of a pilot investigation on the languages of scientific publications, conducted on a sample of Italian scholars belonging to various scientific fields.

Introduction

In this paper we present a review of the main stereotypes concerning English as the language of science, with a special focus on non-Anglophone scholars' perceptions of the reasons behind the predominance of English in scientific literature.

We first discuss the predominance of English in scientific publications in terms of the disadvantages it represents for non-native English speakers, as described by both authors and editors. Secondly, we outline the different explanations given by scholars who have written about English as the language of science. Finally, we discuss data provided by a preliminary survey we conducted at the University of Modena and Reggio Emilia; more specifically we collected up-to-date information on the languages

AILA Review 20 (2007), 28–52. DOI 10.1075/aila.20.05gua
ISSN 1461–0213 / E-ISSN 1570–5595 © John Benjamins Publishing Company

used by Italian-speaking academics for their publications, and on their perception of the role of language in international scientific communication.

1.   English as the language of science: Stereotypes and perceptions

The progressive, "tremendous and unstoppable growth" (Saracino 2004b: 11) of English as the only language of international scientific communication over the last 70 years has been the subject of a great deal of research, driven by different purposes (Ammon 2001a). Such continuous growth has been essentially instantiated by a progressive increase in academic scientific publications in English, along with a corresponding decrease in works published in languages other than English. The phenomenon was initially detected and commented within the so-called "hard" sciences, but recently it has deeply affected even fields pertaining to social sciences and humanities; yet, the current situation (see also the results of the questionnaire in Section 3) shows that the dominance of English is still more evident in hard sciences than in humanities and social sciences. Such tendencies have constantly been monitored through a large amount of statistical analyses on scientific communities belonging to different fields of research and to different native languages (among the others, the pioneer work by Wood 1967, those by Baldauf and Jernudd 1983, Maher 1986, Ammon 1998, Sano 2002, Carli and Calaresu 2003, and also Hamel, this volume).

1.1   Non-Anglophone scholars and the use of English as the language of scientific communication

The increasing dominance of English as the language of international scientific communication[1] has given rise to a considerable growth in English publications written by non-natives; with this respect, the first impressive datum is the under-representation of non-native English-speaking scholars: although the scientific community of native English speakers is smaller than the non-Anglophone one, the proportion of articles produced in English by non-natives — compared to the total amount — is completely reversed: according to several different and independently conducted studies (see above), only about 20% of the global production of English scientific works is produced by non-native speakers.

No statistic is available concerning the specific language background of the authors of the rejected papers, which would be perhaps a further interesting indicator for judging the nature of disadvantages that non-natives face when writing in English. Indeed, one might wonder whether the fact that non-Anglophone scholars publish less English works than their Anglophone (smaller) counterpart is due to mere linguistic inadequateness or whether it is determined by more complex reasons, related for instance to dissimilarities in their cultural traditions or in their scientific background, to the unequal distribution of economic resources for research, and so on.

Thus, another crucial issue arises, "regarding the disadvantage non-native scholars experience in writing for international publications in English compared with their NS[2] peers" (Saracino 2004b: 20). Several studies have shown significant difficulties even for those speakers belonging to language communities with highly-developed second language educational policies.

> Strong anecdotal evidence and occasional references in the literature attest to the disadvantages non-native speakers encounter vis-à-vis their native speaker peers. (Flowerdew 2004b: 201)

Even if their typology varies according to the native language of the speakers, scholars (see for instance Flowerdew 2004 a, b and this volume) have tried to reduce such disadvantages to systematic categories, through the identification of recurrent aspects frequently pointed out by both researchers and editors. This attempt has given rise to the following taxonomy (see also Saracino 2004b):

1. Problems associated to linguistic and discursive aspects: lesser facility of expression, limited vocabulary, difficulty in making claims with the appropriate amount of illocutionary force, simplistic and/or rudimentary stylistic differentiation, anomalous choices in the word order or in the article usage, absence of concord between subject and verb, strategies of deictic marking (Maaß 2006), uncertainty in the use of modals (Hölker 2006) and more generally of hedging strategies (see for instance Diewald 2006, Brauer 2006, Brandt 2006, Siemianov 2006).

2. Difficulties associated with the fact that composing processes are more constrained and laborious for non-native speakers (bigger amount of time needed, influences of the native language, specific parts of the papers which result more "unfriendly" than others, and so on). It has been pointed out by the editors (Flowerdew 2004b) that the most problematic parts for non-native speakers are the introduction and the final discussion, while the sections where methodological issues and results are discussed are less problematic: this is perhaps due to their more formulaic nature (see also Swales 1990).

3. Difficulties associated with cultural differences and different rhetorical traditions: rhetorical patterns are subject to sensible differentiation according to each scholar's cultural background, ideological baggage, and to the communities' cultural practices. This has been studied, for instance, through the perspective of intercultural pragmatics (see for instance Dahl 2004 and Koutsantoni 2005), or of contrastive rhetoric (Mauranen 2004). Such studies have shown that the rhetoric choices which do not conform to the Anglo-Saxon model have less chances to be accepted; in actual fact, different cultural backgrounds seem to give rise to deep differences, affecting not only the stylistic properties of the work but, more significantly, the authoritative credibility of the whole argumentation and, ultimately, its effective impact on the readers' community (Dudley-Evans 1997, Mauranen 2004).

    As far as the stylistic appearance of texts is concerned, the "scientific" genre has been defined both as a "universally" and conventionally definable object, and as a cultural product; indeed, in order to define it, two main sets of properties have been identified (Mauranen 2004):

a. a first relatively uniform set of features imposed by the genre (necessary conditions in order to belong to the scientific argumentative text typology), which are, allegedly, universally defined;

b. a number of individual features essentially related to both intercultural variation and individual authorial choices.

4. Problems caused by material disadvantages and limitations. The discussion of such problems has given rise to a successful field of research, essentially concerning questions related to the social, political and economical dominance of English and of the English-speaking community on the whole. Such issues will not be discussed here as they are debated elsewhere in this volume (see also, for an up to date résumé, Ammon 2006, Carli and Calaresu 2007).

The editors, as revealed by the interviews collected by Flowerdew (2004b), declare an increasing awareness of the obstacles which non-native Anglophones face, agree with the definition of such obstacles, and raise three further problems: the first two respectively address the ability of non-native scholars in stressing the relevance of their own study within the international debate and the difficulties in interpreting the response letters after the refereeing process ("often due to euphemistic models of expression and politeness strategies which can make it difficult for non-native English speaking writers to discern the final decision of the editors, and to understand the revision they would prefer"; Saracino 2004b: 50; see also Canagarajah 2002, 2004). Such disadvantages have been related to difficulties in linguistic choices and partial understanding of the actual intended rhetoric purposes hidden behind such choices. The third issue concerns the lack of authorial voice, which is not directly related to the linguistic background as it affects both native and non-native writers: as editors point out, it is typical of novice writers, independently of their native language (see also Sommers 1980 and St.John 2004).

Even if no official statement exists concerning the editorial strategies to be adopted towards native and non-native English writers, editors manifest a generally positive attitude towards non-natives, along with a number of efforts in order to encourage their publication proposals (such as a more selective choice of reviewers, see again St.John 2004).

According to the interviews and statements which have been published in several different researches (see for instance Saracino 2004a, Part II, and the Modena pilot questionnaire in Section 3), non-Anglophone scholars, despite difficulties and disadvantages, never resent the need to publish in English: using English is conceived as a necessity for anyone who wants to be part of the international scientific debate:

> However, if I can be allowed to be honest, the only reason for my writing the final draft of academic manuscripts in English is that it is almost the only mean of communicating with other scholars in [...] the field where I work professionally. [...] It takes me a long time to complete a refined final draft in English. [...]

> The time difference is quite shocking. Is it still worth the effort to write papers in English? I sometimes wonder. But then I think of the comments I have received from researchers around the world after my papers have been published in international journals. Those are the people I could not have reached if I had not written in English. Their comments have inspired me, and have sometimes opened a whole new world of research to me. (Sasaki 2004: 292–302)

As far as the issue of "time-loss" is concerned, Carli and Calaresu (2007: Section 4) observe that the longer amount of time required by non-Anglophone scholars to write papers in English is not only a matter of amount of hours or money, as it also affects the speed in which the scientific results and discoveries can be spread.

Finally, a further interesting subject in the study of non-native speakers' scientific production has to do with the actual processes of composing a paper in English (Saracino and Calogiuri 2005). Different strategies may be adopted:

1. Writing the paper directly in English and then either submitting it for review by a fluent (native) speaker or not.
2. Writing the paper in the native language (either using the usual scientific style of its speech-community or adopting a simplified "working" variety) and then translating it into English (with or without the help of a fluent speaker). Selecting this option implies a number of difficulties concerning the translator's competence: "the likelihood of a translator being completely fluent in the two languages and also having appropriate scientific knowledge and sensitivity is small" (St.John 2004: 119). Thus, the authors are forced to start a complex process of negotiation and continuous discussion with the translator, and such a process may not always end up with a successful result.

The choice is always guided by the author's self-perceived attitude towards his/her competence in written English, and varies accordingly (see the comments on the Modena questionnaire, Section 3, for a further discussion).

A further, perhaps less discussed issue, pointed out for instance by Baldauf (2001), is about "the other face of the coin", that is about the opportunities for English speakers of writing and publishing papers in languages other than English: it is a well-known and not surprising fact that native English authors constitute a very small set in the non English scientific literature, and that non English publications by Anglophones are mostly related to their authors' specific interests in foreign languages and literature. It is also a fact that English speakers normally do not need to write in languages other than English, but it happens to be true that, when they want to do so, they face the same problems that non-Anglophones encounter when they want to publish in English. Such issues are perhaps not intriguing and less salient within the more general debate on the dominance of English as the language of science, but they might happen to be relevant when facing a more general perspective on the use of foreign languages for purposes of scientific and international communication.

1.2 Why has English become the language of international scientific communication? Stereotypes and *a-posteriori* justifications

In order to explain and justify the increasing dominance of English as the language of international scientific communication, several stereotypes have been created either within the scientific community or externally; these stereotypes have been discussed for the last 30 years within the scientific debate on the "language of science", and have been explained and defined in various ways (see for instance Carli and Calaresu 2007). The traditional stereotypes can essentially be divided into three main typologies:

1. "Internal" justifications

     1a. English is more suitable than any other language to become the only language of science because of its intrinsic properties: it is clearer, easier to learn and more "objective" (see Carli and Calaresu 2007 for the discussion).

     1b. English is more suitable than any other language because it guarantees a "democratic" spread of scientific ideas and a "democratic" expansion of scientific research (see for some discussion Phillipson 2003, Saracino 2004a, Ammon 2006, Carli 2006, van Parjis, Grin and Gazzola this volume). The other face of the "democracy coin" is that, in fact, much as today scholars who do not know English do not have access to the main discoveries of contemporary international scientific research, Anglophone scholars who do not know any national language other than English do not have access to the great deal of scientific traditions developed in the past within national scientific communities (see Carli and Calaresu 2007).

2. "Historical" justifications

     2a. Huge English speaking community (the Americans), especially after the Second World War, has become dominant all over the world in several different domains. Thus, its language has consequently acquired an enormous prestige and power (Brutt-Griffler 2002, Crystal 1997 and 2004, Graddol 1997 and 2004, Ammon 2006, Carli and Calaresu 2007, among the others).

     2b. The status of English as the "universal" language of science is today legitimate much in the same way as that of Latin was in the past (Calaresu 2006 suggests an in-depth updated discussion on these topics, see also Section 2 of this paper).

3. "Practical" justifications

     3a. Regardless of the reasons, English is today the only means of communicating scientific results to the international community and, consequently, to be admitted within such a community; thus, there is no alternative (Ammon 2006).

     3b. The most prestigious international journals only publish in English: even those who are not traditionally related to English-speaking countries/communities have begun to adopt editorial policies which strongly recommend (when not impose) the use of English for publication (Carli and Calaresu 2003, Gaetani 2004 for Italian journals).

It is easy to demonstrate (Carli and Calaresu 2007) that almost all such explanations have been assembled *a-posteriori* in order to legitimize and justify the use and the spread of English, but it is also clear that the "choice" of using English for international scientific communication is not in fact, for non-native speakers, a choice: they feel in some sense obliged to do so, as they know that this is the only way to have access to almost all international scientific networks (for a more accurate discussion, also concerning the role of the "Impact Factor", see Ammon 2006, Calaresu 2006, Carli and Calaresu 2007). Yet, although almost all scholars recognize the "ineluctable necessity" of writing in English, most of them often strongly complain (as seen in Section 1.1) about the difficulties and problems concerning their disadvantaged status with respect to native English speakers: such problems arise both individually and on a broader community-level, as they even affect, for instance, the language teaching and education policies of whole countries. For the purpose of the present review we do not consider issues related to this last point: we will focus on identifying individual behavior, showing how it reflects shared and accepted community attitudes (see also the comments on the Modena questionnaire, Section 3).

2. The non-Anglophone scholars' perception of the predominance of English in scientific literature

Making reference to scientific communication in the broader "continental" sense of the term (for a definition see Carli and Calaresu 2007: 527–28), many books and papers have been written on the use of English for scientific or academic purposes by specialists in language and communication and also, quite interestingly, by academics of other scientific areas, especially belonging to the sub-set of natural sciences as opposed to humanities. In these latter cases, the authors usually offer a series of remarks, or even advice, on the linguistic features that should be present in texts written within the framework of their research sectors (for some examples see Carli and Calaresu 2007: 530).

When accounting for the predominance of English as the language of scientific communication, three main tendencies can be singled out, which we figuratively define as (1) *"matter-of-fact* integrated", (2) *"stereotypically* integrated", and (3) *"critically* integrated".

The "matter-of-fact" integrated scholars simply acknowledge the predominance of English and consider the need for academics to write in English as an inexorable consequence that requires no explanation (see point 3 in Section 1.1). This is often the case in guides and handbooks on academic scientific writing, aimed at non-native speakers and containing indications on the style and structure of academic papers. These works are often translated or converted directly from the same kind of works aimed at native Anglophone speakers and their content is arranged as if the choice of the English language should be as natural and unproblematic for non-native Anglophones as for native Anglophones, a part and parcel of the ingredients for a good scientific paper. An interesting review of Internet resources related to scientific writing can be found on the American Chemical Society Publications site (http://pubs.acs.org/subscribe/jour-nals/ci/31/special/02sb_inet.html, "Internet resources for scientific writing" by Svetla Baykoucheva, manager of the ACS Library and Information Center in Washington, DC), while an exemplary text on the structure of scientific articles directed to non-native Anglophones is Hall (2005), translated from English and already in its third edition in the Italian version.

This matter-of-factness reaches its climax in works arguing against the "quality erosion" of scientific English-language writing. A good example of this attitude can be found in an article published in the *Journal of International Microbiology* (Tychinin and Webb 2003), where the authors (at least one of them working at the Russian Academy of Science and having a non-English first name and surname) criticise the large amount of "words and phrases constantly misused even in reputable international journals", in sum "language errors", collected in the analysis of 155 articles dealing with microbiology, biochemistry, ecology and the environment, plant and soil sciences and written either by scholars with English as L1 (about 30%) or L2 (about 60%) (Tychinin and Webb 2003: 145). Their conclusions consist in a list of recommendations for quality English scientific publications directed to various subjects, i.e. authors, editors, English native speakers and publishers. Native speakers, in particular, should pay special attention to their linguistic use, since they represent the models for non-native English speak-ers, while publishers should not limit themselves to require final editing and revision through the help of a native speaker, since "native speakers are not equally competent to help with the peculiarities of grammar and style" (Tychinin and Webb 2003: 147), and they should add a "professionally compiled 'Hints on Language Use' section to editorial guidelines, identifying common pitfalls of English usage and ways to avoid them. Such a section would occupy a limited amount of printed pages and would be read with profit by non-native speakers of English, especially by those who are not taught courses on sci-entific English writing in their home countries" (Tychinin and Webb 2003: 148). Apart from the still questionable advantages that such a solution might imply for non-native English authors, it also seems to suggest that the property of the scientific language sim-ply consists of the use of specific words and phrases (see Calaresu 2006: 43–7).

The undisputed acceptance of the dominance of English is often connected with the view that English is becoming the universal language of science in the same way as Latin has been in the past, without taking into account the impressive amount of differences (Calaresu 2006: 48–57).

According to a second group of scholars, those that we have defined as "ste-reotypically integrated", the predominance of English can be justified by means of its alleged structural "simplicity", which would make it at the same time a very easy language to learn and a sort of ideal implement for conveying concepts in scientific communication.

A peculiar example of this tendency is provided by Calaresu (2006: 48–9) and Carli and Calaresu (2007: 533–5), who mention the book *Doing Science*, written by the bi-ologist Ivan Valiela, a non-native English speaker (Valiela 2001). In the perspective of providing the "essentials of what practicing scientists need to know about (1) asking, (2) testing, and (3) communicating results about a scientific question, above and beyond the knowledge they might need about specific fields of study" (Valiela 2001: v), the author dedicates two sections to "the matter of which language to use" and to "writing scientific English" respectively. In the first section, he explains that the predominance of English as the language of science is due to economic affluence and number of speakers, but also to *relative ease of use* ("its grammar is relatively easy to learn"), *brevity* ("an unexpected feature, considering its voluminous vocabulary" that allows us "to say something in fewer words using English than in many other languages"), and *large vocabulary* ("it has the largest vocabulary of any language, readily adopts new terms"). The explanations provided for this point reveals the naive and simplistic linguistic assumptions at the basis of the argumentation: "there is little concern among English speakers about maintaining purity of the language. English has been a flexible language that pragmatically adopts many terms", and, in order to demonstrate this, the author provides a list of English words borrowed from diverse languages, such as *alcohol, atoll, bungalow, oasis, poncho* and *tundra* (Valiela 2001: 104–106), without mentioning that they have been adopted with the same flexibility by most European languages. In the section entitled "Scientific writing in English", then, Valiela summarises "the four major features that determine if a scientific paper is murky or effectively communicates its message: word use, sentence structure, paragraph structure, and organization of the parts of the paper" (Valiela 2001: 108). Admittedly, the paragraph is intended merely as an introduction to general concepts that might result problematic, while "for rules about writing in general there is no better guide (or shorter, only 92 pages!) than the classic "little book" *The Elements of Style* by Strunk and White (1979)" (Valiela 2001: 108).

This idea that English is the most appropriate vehicle for scientific writing recalls the fascinating ideal of a perfect language, which, in spite of its very long tradition and its almost continuous presence in the imagination of *homo loquens* since the very beginning (for an interesting review, see Swiggers 2001), has, unfortunately, proved possible only in a mythical perspective. Again Calaresu (2006: 39–47) and Carli and Calaresu (2007: 540–43) have analysed various aspects of the concept of the so called universal language of science underlining its different problematic aspects and showing that it cannot be referred to a specific language, but to a certain use of any natural language.

Finally, one might even accept, to a certain extent, that some morpho-syntactic aspects of English and the possibility to use a lexicon derived from Latin and Greek could make English easier to learn — or use — than other non-native languages, at least for Europeans. However, the most relevant problem, often ignored in this kind of literature (but discussed and clearly motivated in Hyland 1997, 2000, 2004, Calaresu 2006, Carli and Calaresu 2007, Saracino and Calogiuri 2005), is the argumentative competence required to be able to write a scientific article, given that the rhetorical conventions of a language are much more difficult to learn than a list of words or syntactic structures (as seen in Section 1.1. above). With this respect, Carli and Calaresu (2007: 538–40) review some studies concerning the organization of information and the rhetorical-stylistic dimension of academic writing in the framework of the connections between academic communities and their texts.

Another interesting field of research related to these aspects concerns the studies of international and intercultural communication in English, which try to provide an analysis of non-native English varieties (see for instance Wolf and Polzenhagen 2006 or House 2003). House (2003), in particular, after distinguishing between *language for communication* and *language for identification*, reports data from research projects carried out at Hamburg University aimed at analysing the features of the English language used for communication by non-native speakers, as well as the impact of English on discourse norms, for instance in terms of information structure or word order of the local languages used alongside English.

Only a third group of scholars, the "critically integrated", explicitly links the predominance of English for scientific communication to economic reasons (de Swaan 2001, Ammon 2006, Calaresu 2006, Carli and Calaresu 2007 and Hamel, this volume). Ammon (2006), for instance, describes the choice of English as the sole international scientific language as tightly interconnected with the increasingly unlimited globalisation of science and with the shift that has taken place from a situation characterised by different equally important scientific centres, for the different kinds of disciplines, to one single centre: the United States. This centre has the wealthiest and biggest scientific market, which also means that publishing scientific works within this context gives prestige to authors and to the institutions they belong to. This same market imposes the use of its own language, but this is usually accepted by non-native speakers of English as an inevitable cost, in terms of both money and energy, in order to have the possibility of publishing within this context. In this perspective, even if the choice of the language is made by the individual scientist or scholar, various factors influence this choice. Some of the conditions for being included in the Citation Indexes, such as the use of English, but also the activity of referencing (which is usually done in English), strengthen this mechanism for the authors, as well as for the members of editorial boards. The process becomes circular when the Indexes, for which the use of English is recommended, are then used to demonstrate the predominance of English as the language of science.

3. How do Italian-speaking scholars perceive the predominance of English within international scientific communication? Evidence from a pilot study

In order to provide a further perspective on the actual behavior of the non-Anglophone scientific community with regards to the dominance of English, a pilot investigation was conducted on a small selected sample of Italian-speaking scholars, belonging to a heterogeneous set of research areas (see Table 1: the sample is quite different, with this respect, from that collected by Saracino and Calogiuri 2005, uniquely consisting of scholars belonging to the fields of Economics, Statistics, Mathematics and Law), and all working within at least one of the following academic institutions at the University of Modena and Reggio Emilia:

–   Department of Social, Cognitive and Quantitative Sciences
–   Department of Language and Cultural Sciences
–   Faculty of Communication Sciences and Economics
–   Faculty of Educational Sciences
–   Faculty of Economics
–   Faculty of Humanities
–   Faculty of Law
–   Faculty of Medicine

Informants were asked to answer an anonymous ten-question questionnaire, either in electronic or paper format. 125 questionnaires were collected in sum.

The questionnaire consists of the following questions.[3]

1.   How many of the scientific works you've published or submitted since 2004 are in English? How many in Italian? How many in other languages?

The first question has a merely quantitative nature: it explores whether the scientific production by the scholars of the sample has an "international" character or not. The results are collected in Table 2 and Table 3, which essentially show that, as expected,

Table 1. Scientific areas

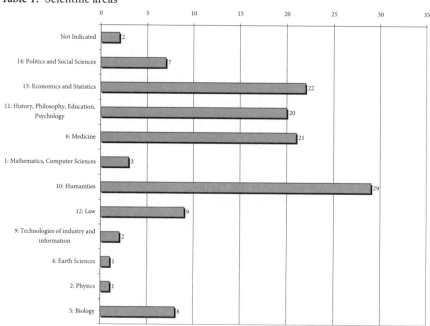

Italian and English are the two most used languages (Table 2) and that, again as expected, in the scientific areas which can be included in so-called "hard sciences" the language of publication is almost exclusively English (Table 3). A further interesting datum, that is essentially in line with those proposed by Carli and Calaresu (2003) and Gaetani (2004), is that even in the so called "social" and "human sciences" the use of English happens to be in expansion (36 over 58 informants declare that more than 25% of their scientific publications is in English). The result essentially confirms the general well-described tendency of a progressive spread of English as the language of

Table 2. Scientific publications: languages

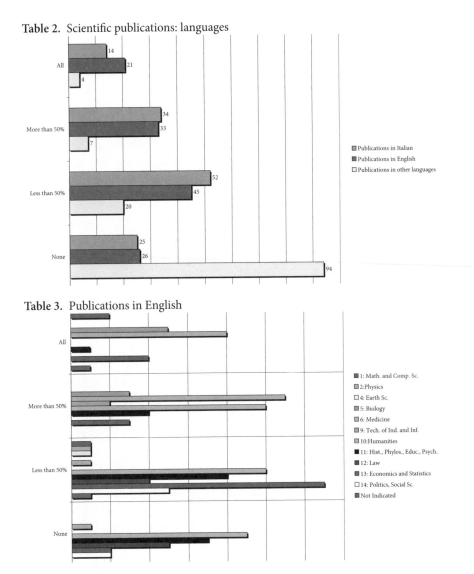

Table 3. Publications in English

scientific publications, even in those areas which have traditionally been more reluctant to adopt it.

2. If you have submitted any publication in English, what has been the main reason? (more than one answer is accepted). *the editor only accepts works in English / the editor only accepts works in languages other than Italian / I thought that writing in English was better / I prefer writing in English / English is the language I normally use for my scientific publications*

The question aims to elicit an explicit statement on the reasons for the use of English, and the answers clearly show, again, what the scientific literature has already pointed out (see Section 1.2. in this paper): writing in English is almost never a real choice; Italian scholars do not "prefer" writing in English (1.4%), they sometimes think that writing in English might be better than using any other language (17.4%), but more often they are forced by the editorial policies (50.8%) and, even more explicitly, by the need of inclusion in the international scientific network: quite a large number of informants (30.4%) simply states that English is the language that they normally use for their publications, as if to underline the acceptance of its predominance for academic writing as a matter-of-fact (see also Section 2 in this paper; in particular, this has been the answer preferred by those who belong to the medical and biological sectors: as far as the medical area is concerned, the penetration of English in the Italian journals of Medicine is discussed and commented in Carli and Calaresu 2003: 45–58).

3. How relevant do you think it is, in order for a scholar of your discipline to get international visibility and to spread his/her works and ideas around the international community, that his/her works are written in English? *of great importance and necessity/ of great importance and to be wished/ relatively important/ of no importance*

Here, again, informants are asked to reflect on the very reasons behind their "choice" of using English (or not to do so), and to motivate it on the basis of the scientific environment in which they live and work. Therefore, we expect that the answers to the first three questions are internally coherent. Table 5 sums up the results: as expected, scholars belonging to those scientific areas which show a higher quantity of publications in English (Medicine, Biology, Economics and Statistics, see Table 3) declare the high degree of importance and necessity in using English, while those who still maintain a balance, at least between English and Italian (Humanities, Politics and Social Sciences, Law), spread more heterogeneously across the four answers.

4. When you write a work in a language other than Italian (more than one answer is accepted)…: *I write it in that language and then I send it to the editor without any native speaker's review / I write it in that language and then, before sending it to the editor, I ask for a review by a native speaker / I write it in Italian and then I translate it myself without any native speaker's review / I write it in Italian, I translate it by*

myself, and then, before sending it to the editor, I ask for a review by a native speaker / I write it in Italian and then I ask for a translation by a native speaker.

Table 4. Scientific Areas, Question 2

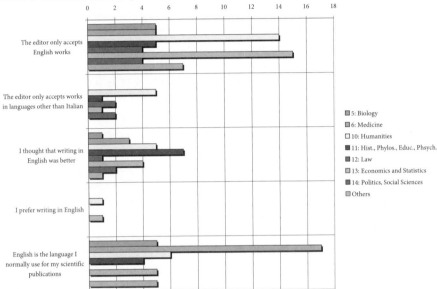

Table 5. Scientific Areas, Question 3

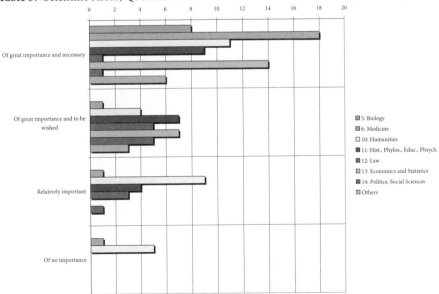

Question 4 explores the attitude of non-native scholars towards writing in English (see St.John 2004, Saracino and Calogiuri 2005), in order to examine how this scientific community deals with the problem of rigorously showing the results of high level scientific works using a non-native language; this problem raises several interesting issues, such as those concerning the costs of publishing in languages other than their own native one (Halliday 2004, Carli 2006, Carli and Calaresu 2007, Felloni 2006, Van Parjis, this volume) and the politics of foreign language teaching even in academic environments (see for these issues the *Journal of English for Academic Purposes*, edited by Liz Hamp Lyons and Ken Hyland, Pergamon).

It would not be a mistake to assume that almost all the scholars of our sample show a receptive competence in reading English: they declare that at least a half of the scientific works they usually read is in English (cf. question 8). Furthermore, the answers to question 10 show that even their self-perception of their competence in English is of a middle/high level. Considering such facts, the attitudes towards writing in languages other than Italian (English, for the most part of our informants) which emerge from the answers to this question are coherent (see Table 6): scholars tend to write their papers directly in the "final" language (80%), and not all of them happen to need any revision by native speakers (61.3% ask for an expert reviewer). As for those who prefer to write in Italian first (the remaining 20%), the majority asks for the help of a reviewer (54.8%) or of a translator (35.5%).

When we look more in detail at the scientific areas (Table 7) we notice, again, that scholars belonging to Medicine and Biology uniformly declare that they write in English, while those belonging to Humanities and social areas are spread more

Table 6. Question 4

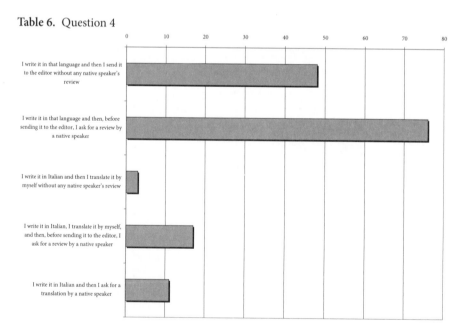

heterogeneously. Quite interestingly, 9 out of 28 scholars belonging to Economics and Statistics, while declaring a high competence in English (question 10), a high quantity of works read in English (question 8) and a high percentage of works published in English (question 1), thus allowing one to hypothesize a high competence even in writing, unexpectedly reveal the custom of having their works translated by others (native speakers). Given such differences, the results are essentially in line with those proposed by St.John (2004) in her study on Spanish-speaking scholars' writing strategies and with Saracino and Calogiuri's research on Italian speaking scholars (2005).

The next three questions explicitly concern one of the more debated issues in this field: non-Anglophone scholars often complain of an enormous difficulty for their works to be accepted by international journals and editors. This is due to a lack of native competence in English, that is a lack of fluency and ability in using suitable linguistic and stylistic constructions, a lack of ability in the choice of rhetoric strategies and of expertise in giving the appropriate strength to their claims, and so on (see Section 1.1. in this paper). According to statistics, English works written by non-natives are fewer than those written by natives; nevertheless, according to Flowerdew (2004b), the editors are perfectly aware of such difficulties, and try to consider them in evaluating submissions by non-natives. The picture happens to be so intricate — as both authors and editors point out — due to the absence of any international guideline, which establishes some sort of standard format representing the "zero degree" of scientific writing, i.e. the basic shape of a scientific paper in order to be considered for international publication: such a lack of a universal standard model of the scientific genre (Mauranen 2004) has been largely debated (see for a summary Calaresu 2006

Table 7. Scientific Areas, Question 4

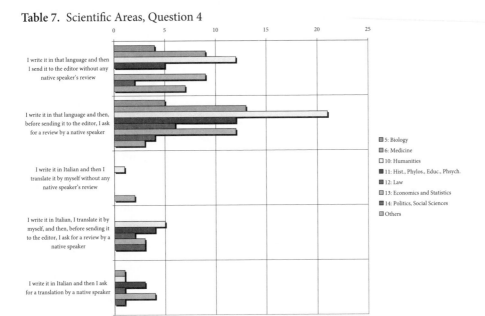

and Guardiano 2006), leading to the conclusion that, perhaps for principled reasons, such an ideal model will never exist (as the answers to the next question largely confirm). It is however worth pointing out that those scholars who experienced a specific and systematic education in writing academic works in English (i.e. attending specific seminars and classes) declare a higher degree of acceptance than their colleagues (see the essays in Saracino 2004a).

5. Have you ever received, before sending a work in English to a journal or an editor, any explicit guideline concerning the stylistic and/or formal shape of the text (except for the style-sheet)? *yes/no*

Table 8 shows that the majority of scholars, regardless of their disciplines, confirms the absence of explicit models (one partial exception is represented by biologists and by scholars belonging to Politics and Social Sciences: quite a half of them declare to have received explicit guidelines).

6. Have you ever received, after submitting a work to a journal or an editor, any explicit suggestion concerning the stylistic and/or formal shape of the text? *never/ at least one time/ sometimes/ often/ always*

Table 9 shows that, as expected, the stylistic, rhetorical and linguistic review of English works produced by non-native speakers is quite rigorous: approximately a half out of the total amount of informants declare that they received explicit stylistic and formal suggestions; yet, such a brief question cannot give any idea of the comments usually given by the reviewers to non-native speakers, of the changes more often required, and of the differences (if any) with respect to those proposed to native ones: a deeper qualitative investigation would be needed in order to sketch a more precise picture.

7. Have any of your works ever been judged negatively by any editorial committee only because of an inadequate stylistic and/or formal shape of the text? *yes/ no*

The answers confirm Flowerdew's (2004b) findings, i.e. editors tend not to exclude non-native speakers' works only because of shortcomings in their formal skills, even if it is just as clear that non-native speakers must face longer and more complicate procedures than their native peers in order to have their works accepted for international publication. This is perhaps an unsolvable question, that might probably be mitigated by more accurate and attentive efforts to develop, define and spread more feasible guidelines in order to give non-native speakers useful and reliable tools for balancing such an *a-priori* default. Such guidelines in fact already exist, coming from the practice of offering specific courses on "writing in English for academic and scientific purpose", firmly rooted in several Anglophone academic institutions.

> In order to raise awareness of these problems I have postulated [...] the 'non-native speakers' right to linguistic peculiarities. It may appear a rather hopeless postulate considering the well-founded linguistic veneration of the native speaker,

but I believe it deserves closer examination, also [the] possibilities of a political campaign to gather support similar to that for female linguistic rights. [...] I am aware that the postulate of equity for non-native speakers of English, to put it another way, faces far more formidable obstacles than did, or does, linguistic gender neutrality. It needs, first of all, adequate specification before it can be taken seriously (Ammon 2001b: vii–viii).

Table 8. Scientific areas, Question 5

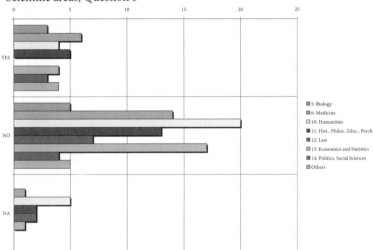

Table 9. Scientific areas, Question 6

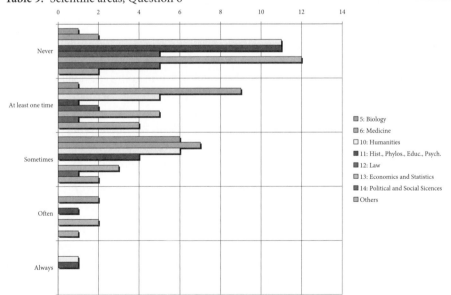

Table 10. Scientific areas, Question 7

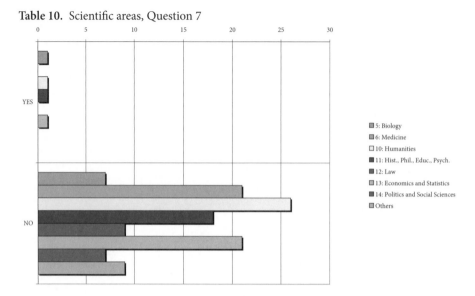

The two following questions are one the counterpart of the other: they both aim to verify the role of English within each single research area (and for this specific purpose are to be compared to the first three questions of the questionnaire) and to give an idea of the competence of the informants in reading papers in English.

8. How many of the scientific papers you've read during the last three years were in English? *more than 50%/ about 50%/ less than 50%*

9. How many of the scientific papers you've read during the last three years were in languages other than English? *more than 50%/ about 50%/ less than 50%*

The results seem to confirm our previous observations: scholars whose publications are mainly written in English read works in English (Medicine, Economy, Statistics) while those who also write in languages other than English (Humanities and Social Sciences) include many more languages (besides Italian, they often cite German, French and Spanish) in their readings.

Finally, the last question has been conceived as a sort of counterproof, in order to see whether the informants' explicit answers on their competence are in line with the implicit ones concerning the very use of English in their research activity.

10. How do you evaluate your own competence in English? *no problems/ I can do it/ I do it, but it isn't easy/ I'm not able*

The most interesting datum is that scholars belonging to the field of Humanities declare the highest level of competence. Such an apparent anomaly presumably depends on the fact that several scholars belonging to the field of Humanities are bilingual, and thus have specific expertise in English language and literature. More generally, the

Table 11. Scientific areas, Question 8 (English)

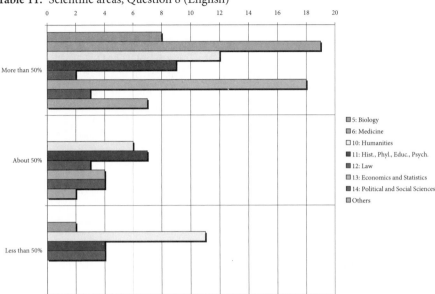

claim of good competence in English, even for those who have not declared publications in that language, might be interpreted in the light of the general acceptance of the predominance of the use of English and the fear of resulting inadequate in admitting a scarce competence in writing in English.

4.   Conclusions

In this paper we outlined the current predominance of English as the language of science, focusing on the disadvantages for non-Anglophone scholars, on their perception about such matters, and on the stereotypes and *a-posteriori* justifications for the predominance of English. In the last section, we presented the results of a pilot investigation conducted on a sample of Italian scholars belonging to various scientific fields.

As expected, English proves to be not only the language used almost exclusively for publishing in the "hard sciences" but is also increasingly requested in "social" and "human sciences". Writing in English is nonetheless perceived by non-Anglophone scholars as a sort of ineluctable necessity (related to both international prestige and editorial needs) rather than a matter of free choice.

Such tendencies can easily be explained as epiphenomena of the more complex phenomenon concerning the absolute dominance of English on the international language market, which in turn depends on even more complex mechanisms affecting the international economic market as a whole (Warsh 2006, Grin & Gazzola, this volume, van Parjis, this volume).

On the other hand, the increasing dominance of English has been discussed by non-experts (in language and/or communication sciences), i.e. scientists who increasingly use English for scientific and academic purposes but which, at the same time, feel the need to justify such a "choice". As these scholars are usually not aware of the sociolinguistic debate about these topics (see Sections 1 and 2) and of the complex

Table 12. Scientific areas, Question 9 (other than English)

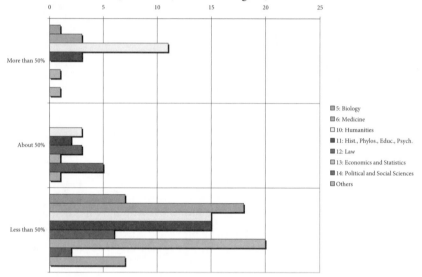

Table 13. Scientific areas, Question 10

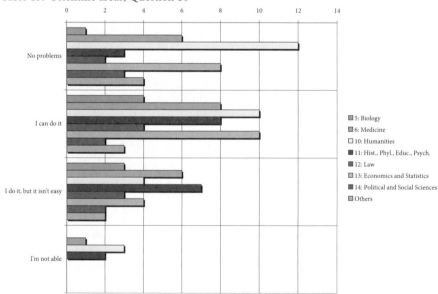

relations of cause and effect between promoting monolingualism or multilingualism both in society and in science, they often significantly (and unwittingly) contribute to increasing the amount of stereotypes and justifications, which emerge exponentially as the debate becomes more intense.

In sum, bias and stereotypes about English seem to emerge both from expert and non-expert opinions. But, of course, no easy answer to the problems posed by the dominance of English can be satisfactorily provided unless we overcome the same stereotyped dichotomy of English as a "language killer" and English as a kind of "communicative cure-all". We have by now an adequate amount of literature on the causes and consequences of a growing monolingualism in scientific communication, and it is perhaps high time to soundly consider and scrutinize feasible and democratic solutions (such as actively promoting receptive multilingualism, granting non-native rights to linguistic peculiarities, etc.) in order to reduce and remove non-native disadvantages in scientific communication as well as in those other contexts where international communication is involved.

Notes

* We are indebted to Augusto Carli for his precious suggestions throughout the elaboration of this work, and to two anonymous referees for their inspiring comments. The paper, in its final form, is the result of a collaboration between the three authors. Cristina Guardiano is directly responsible for Sections 1 and 3, M.Elena Favilla for Section 2, Emilia Calaresu supervised the whole writing process; the introduction and the conclusions were written jointly.

1. For a detailed discussion on the problems raised by the spread of English as the international language of scientific publications, see also the papers presented at the ESOF (Euroscience Open Forum) 2004 Symposium on "Spreading the word: who profits from scientific publications?", available at: http://www.esof2004.org/pdf_ppt/session_material/praderie_cover.pdf.

2. NS = native speakers.

3. The whole dataset and its consequent statistical elaboration are available on Cristina Guardiano's homepage: http://cdm.unimo.it/home/dipslc/guardiano.cristina. The data in the tables refer to the number of interviewees, and never express any percentage.

References

Ammon, U. 1998. *Ist Deutsch noch internationale Wissenschaftssprache? English auch für die Lehre an den deutschsprachigen Hochschulen.* Berlin: Mouton de Gruyter.
Ammon, U. (ed.). 2001a. *The Dominance of English as a Language of Science. Effects on other languages and language communities.* Berlin: Mouton de Gruyter.
Ammon, U. 2001b. Editor's Preface. In Ammon 2001a, v–x.

Ammon, U. 2006. Language planning for international scientific communication: an overview of questions and potential solutions. *Current Issues in Language Planning* 7(1): 1–30.

Baldauf, R.B. & Jernudd, B.H. 1983. Language of publications as a variable in scientific communication. *Australian Review of Applied Linguistics* 6(1): 97–108.

Baldauf, R.B. 2001. Speaking of Science. The use by Australian university science staff of language skills. In Ammon 2001a, 139–165.

Brandt, D. 2006. Heckenausdrücke in Einleitungen zu *Tesi di laurea*. In *Italienisch und Deutsch als Wissentschaftsprachen. Bestandsaufnahmen, Analysen, Perspektiven. / Italiano e Tedesco come lingue della comunicazione scientifica. Ricognizioni, Analisi, Prospettive*, E. Calaresu, C. Guardiano & K. Hölker (eds.), 277–294, Münster: LIT Verlag.

Brauer, E. 2006. Hecken in Einleitungen zu wissenschaftlichen Abschlussarbeiten. In *Italienisch und Deutsch als Wissentschaftsprachen. Bestandsaufnahmen, Analysen, Perspektiven. / Italiano e Tedesco come lingue della comunicazione scientifica. Ricognizioni, Analisi, Prospettive*, E. Calaresu, C. Guardiano & K. Hölker (eds.), 261–275, Münster: LIT Verlag.

Brutt-Griffler, J. 2002. *World English. A study of its development*. Clevedon: Multilingual Matters.

Calaresu, E. 2006. L'universalità del linguaggio scientifico fra norma d'uso e sistema linguistico. Plurilinguismo e monolinguismo nella comunicazione scientifica. In *Italienisch und Deutsch als Wissentschaftsprachen. Bestandsaufnahmen, Analysen, Perspektiven. / Italiano e Tedesco come lingue della comunicazione scientifica. Ricognizioni, Analisi, Prospettive*, E. Calaresu, C. Guardiano & K. Hölker (eds.), 29–64, Münster: LIT Verlag.

Canagarajah, A.S. 2002. *A Geopolitics of Academic Writing*. Pittsburgh PA: UniPress.

Canagarajah, A.S. 2004. Nondiscursive requirements in academic publishing, material resources of periphery scholars, and the politics of knowledge production. In Saracino 2006a, 241–287.

Carli, A. 2006. La questione linguistica nella comunicazione scientifica oggi in Italia e in Germania. In *Italienisch und Deutsch als Wissentschaftsprachen. Bestandsaufnahmen, Analysen, Perspektiven. / Italiano e Tedesco come lingue della comunicazione scientifica. Ricognizioni, Analisi, Prospettive*, E. Calaresu, C. Guardiano & K. Hölker (eds.), 101–137, Münster: LIT Verlag.

Carli, A. & Calaresu, E. 2003. Le lingue della comunicazione scientifica. La produzione e la diffusione del sapere specialistico in Italia. In *Ecologia linguistica*, A. Valentini, P. Molinelli, P. Cuzzolin & G. Bernini (eds.), 27–74, Roma: Bulzoni.

Carli, A. & Calaresu, E. 2007. Language and Science. In *Handbook of Language and Communication: Diversity and change* [Handbook of Applied Linguistics 9], M. Hellinger & A. Pauwels (eds.), 523–551, Berlin: de Gruyter.

Crystal, D. 1997. *English as a Global Language*, 2nd edn., 2003. Cambridge: CUP.

Crystal, D. 2004. *La rivoluzione delle lingue*. Bologna: Il Mulino.

Dahl, T. 2004. Textual metadiscourse in research articles: a marker of national culture or of academic discourse? *Journal of Pragmatics* 36: 1807–1825.

de Swaan, A. 2001. *Words of the World. The Global Language System*. Cambridge: Polity Press.

Diewald, G. 2006. Hecken und Heckenausdrücke. Versuch einer Neuedefinition. In *Italienisch und Deutsch als Wissentschaftsprachen. Bestandsaufnahmen, Analysen, Perspektiven. / Italiano e Tedesco come lingue della comunicazione scientifica. Ricognizioni, Analisi, Prospettive*, E. Calaresu, C. Guardiano & K. Hölker (eds.), 295–315, Münster: LIT Verlag.

Dudley-Evans, T. 1997. Genre: how far can we, should we go? *World Englishes* 16: 351–358.

Felloni, M.C. 2006. Principi della politica linguistica europea fra teoria e prassi. Ripercussioni sulla comunicazione scientifica. In *Italienisch und Deutsch als Wissentschaftsprachen. Be-*

standsaufnahmen, Analysen, Perspektiven. / Italiano e Tedesco come lingue della comunicazione scientifica. Ricognizioni, Analisi, Prospettive, E. Calaresu, C. Guardiano & K. Hölker (eds.), 65–100, Münster: LIT Verlag.

Flowerdew, J. 2004a. Problems in writing for scholarly publication in English: The case of Hong Kong. In Saracino 2004a, 81–113.

Flowerdew, J. 2004b. Attitudes of journal editors to nonnative speaker contributions. In Saracino 2004a, 201–240.

Gaetani, S. 2004. *Le lingue della comunicazione scientifica. Uno studio su riviste italiane di Biologia e Sociologia*. Modena: Università di Modena e Reggio Emilia (Tesi del Corso di Laurea in Lingue e Culture Europee, Facoltà di Lettere e Filosofia). Summary available at: http://www.linguaggioecultura.unimo.it/materiali.php?uplink=0.

Graddol, D. 1997. *The Future of English*. London: The British Council.

Graddol, D. 2004. The future of language. *Science* 303: 1329–1330.

Guardiano, C. 2006. Mutamento e contatto linguistico: considerazioni sulle lingue della comunicazione scientifica. In *Italienisch und Deutsch als Wissentschaftsprachen. Bestandsaufnahmen, Analysen, Perspektiven. / Italiano e Tedesco come lingue della comunicazione scientifica. Ricognizioni, Analisi, Prospettive*, E. Calaresu, C. Guardiano & K. Hölker (eds.), 139–176. Münster: LIT Verlag.

Hall, G.M. 2005. *Come scrivere un lavoro scientifico*, 3rd edn., Torino: Minerva medica.

Halliday, M.A.K. 2004. *The Language of Science*. London: Continuum.

Hölker, K. 2006. Verben im wissenschaftlichen Texten. In *Italienisch und Deutsch als Wissentschaftsprachen. Bestandsaufnahmen, Analysen, Perspektiven. / Italiano e Tedesco come lingue della comunicazione scientifica. Ricognizioni, Analisi, Prospettive*, E. Calaresu, C. Guardiano & K. Hölker (eds.), 195–224, Münster: LIT Verlag.

House, J. 2003. English as a lingua franca: A threat to multilingualism? *Journal of Sociolinguistics* 7: 556–578.

Hyland, K. 1997. Scientific claims and community values: Articulating an academic culture. *Language & Communication* 17(1): 19–31.

Hyland, K. 2000. *Disciplinary Discourses: Social interaction in academic writing*. London: Longman.

Hyland, K. 2004. *Genre and Second Language Writing*. Ann Arbor MI: The University of Michigan Press.

Koutsantoni, D. 2005. Certainty across cultures: A comparison of the degree of certainty expressed by Greek and English speaking scientific authors. *Intercultural Pragmatics* 2(2): 121–149.

Maaß, C. 2006. Diskursdeixis in Einleitungen zu wissenschaftlichen Abschlussarbeiten deutscher und italienischer Studierender. In *Italienisch und Deutsch als Wissentschaftsprachen. Bestandsaufnahmen, Analysen, Perspektiven. / Italiano e Tedesco come lingue della comunicazione scientifica. Ricognizioni, Analisi, Prospettive*, E. Calaresu, C. Guardiano & K. Hölker (eds.), 225–260, Münster: LIT Verlag.

Maher, J. 1986. The development of English as the international language of medicine. *Applied Linguistics* 7: 201–218.

Mauranen, A. 2004. Contrastive ESP rhetoric: metatext in Finnish-English economics tests. In Saracino 2004a, 126–156.

Phillipson, R. 2003. *English-Only Europe? Challenging language policy*. London: Routledge.

Sano, H. 2002. The world's lingua franca of science. *English Today* 18: 45–49.

Saracino, G.M. (ed.) 2004a. *Writing for Scholarly Publication in English*. Lecce: Manni.

Saracino, G.M. 2004b. Introduction. In Saracino 2004a, 11–77.

Saracino, G.M. & Calogiuri, A. 2005. Problemi nella scrittura di articoli scientifici in inglese da parte di studiosi italiani. In *Atti del 5° Congresso Internazionale dell'Associazione Italiana di Linguistica Applicata*, E. Banfi, L. Gavioli, C. Guardiano & M. Vedovelli (eds.), 305–343, Perugia: Guerra.

Sasaki, M. 2004. An introspective account of L2 writing acquisition. In Saracino 2004a, 291–304.

Siemianow, B. 2006. Reformulierungen in wissenschaftlichen Texten und der Gebrauch von *cioè*. In *Italienisch und Deutsch als Wissentschaftsprachen. Bestandsaufnahmen, Analysen, Perspektiven. / Italiano e Tedesco come lingue della comunicazione scientifica. Ricognizioni, Analisi, Prospettive*, E. Calaresu, C. Guardiano & K. Hölker (eds.), 317–336, Münster: LIT.

Sommers, N. 1980. Revision strategies of students writers and experienced adult writers. *College Composition and Communication* 31: 378–388.

St.John, M.J. 2004. Writing processes of Spanish scientists publishing in English. In Saracino 2004a, 114–125.

Swales, J. 1990. *Genre Analysis. English in Academic and Research Settings*. Cambridge: CUP.

Swiggers, P. 2001. L'idée de langue universelle et de langue parfaite dans l'histoire de la linguistique occidentale. In *Storia del pensiero linguistico: linearità, fratture e circolarità*. Atti del Convegno della Società Italiana di Glottologia, Verona 11–13 novembre 1999, G. Massariello Merzagora (ed.), 13–46, Roma: Il Calamo.

Tychinin, D. N. & Webb, V.A. 2003. Confused and misused: English under attack in scientific literature. *International Microbiology* 6: 145–148.

Valiela, I. 2003. *Doing Science. Design, analysis, and communication of scientific research*. Oxford: OUP.

Warsh, D. 2006. *Knowledge and the Wealth of Nations. A story of economic discovery*. New York NY: W.W. Norton.

Wolf, H.-G. & Polzenhagen, F. 2006. Intercultural communication in English: Arguments for a cognitive approach to intercultural pragmatics. *Intercultural Pragmatics* 3(3): 285–321.

Wood, D.N. 1967. The foreign language problem facing scientists and technologists in the United Kingdom: report of a recent survey. *Journal of Documentation 23*: 117–130.

Authors' address

Dipartimento di Scienze del Linguaggio e della Cultura
Università di Modena e Reggio Emilia
Largo Sant'Eufemia 19
I-41100 Modena

Cristina Guardiano: cristina.guardiano@unimore.it
M. Elena Favilla: elena.favilla@unimore.it
Emilia Calaresu: emilia.calaresu@unimore.it

The dominance of English in the international scientific periodical literature and the future of language use in science

Rainer Enrique Hamel
Universidad Autónoma Metropolitana, México, D. F.

Throughout the 20th century, international communication has shifted from a plural use of several languages to a clear pre-eminence of English, especially in the field of science. This paper focuses on international periodical publications where more than 75 percent of the articles in the social sciences and humanities and well over 90 percent in the natural sciences are written in English. The shift towards English implies that an increasing number of scientists whose mother tongue is not English have already moved to English for publication. Consequently, other international languages, namely French, German, Russian, Spanish and Japanese lose their attraction as languages of science. Many observers conclude that it has become inevitable to publish in English, even in English only. The central question is whether the actual hegemony of English will create a total monopoly, at least at an international level, or if changing global conditions and language policies may allow alternative solutions. The paper analyses how the conclusions of an inevitable monopoly of English are constructed, and what possible disadvantages such a process might entail. Finally, some perspectives of a new plurilingual approach in scientific production and communication are sketched.

1. Introduction. What is at stake in the field?

Even two or three decades ago, this article could have been published in this very journal, the AILA Review, in English or French, AILA's official languages, or even in German or Russian, two languages that were then accepted as congress languages. When AILA was founded and held its first congress in 1964, it was formed overwhelmingly by foreign language and translation experts and it promoted enrichment plurilingualism which meant the daily bread for its members. Its acronym is indeed coined on its name in French, *Association Internationale de Linguistique Appliquée,* the then leading language of the association. Things have changed since, and, at least from 2003 onwards,

AILA Review 20 (2007), 53–71. DOI 10.1075/aila.20.06ham
ISSN 1461–0213 / E-ISSN 1570–5595 © John Benjamins Publishing Company

the AILA Review has become an 'English only' publication. The authors' guidelines I received establish that "articles should be written in English". Should? Volume 16 (2003) to 19 (2006) do not contain a single article that is not written in English. This shift represents a trend that has developed over the 20th century as part and parcel of a more global language shift process in the international arena of scientific publication.

In the context of dynamic changes in global multilingualism, present day international and national communication in science can be framed within a sociolinguistic conflict model of asymmetric relationships and shift between languages on specific levels of a hierarchy that represent differentiated power relations in the field of science. De Swaan (1993, 2001) designed a hierarchical model of the global world system as a galaxy of languages: English is today's sole globally dominant language, the "hyper-central" language of the world. On the second level we find less than a dozen "super-central" languages among which are French, Spanish, Russian, Chinese, Japanese, Arabic, Hindi, German and Portuguese. Many of them represent languages of former colonial or regional empires and are spoken in more than one country. The third level is occupied by approximately a hundred "central" languages, often national or significant regional languages with little or no international diffusion. The vast majority of the world's languages, some 98 per cent, belong to the fourth level of the "peripheral" or vernacular languages, which are the mother tongues of usually small ethnic groups but hold no official status in the countries where they are spoken. No wonder vernacular languages almost never appear in the debates about languages in science, since their status and corpus are considered unfit to express scientific thought and research findings. Significant changes in the appreciation of what constitutes scientific thought, however, as e.g. the profound knowledge about biological and agricultural processes enshrined in indigenous languages, have brought about a change in focus. Furthermore, many indigenous or intercultural universities founded in Latin America and other parts of the world increasingly seek to equip indigenous languages for academic work (Skutnabb-Kangas 2004).

Until the end of World War I English belonged to the small group of leading international languages. Once English had gained a significant lead over its competitors during World War II (Kaplan 2001), a new category had to be introduced that pointed to the new status of English. The fundamental language conflict and shift process that has occupied language globalization debates on the international scene focuses on the course of action by which English is expanding its international domains, thus pushing all super-central languages into the role of central languages and absorbing their functions in many if not most international arenas. Should this process come to fruition, English would become the sole language of communication between other language communities above the state level in most areas. Such a state of affairs coincides with Crystal's (1997) model of world bilingualism: everyone speaks her or his own language and at the same time English as the only foreign language. As a matter of fact, there has never been a language as dominant as English in history, whose role may however decline again during the 21st century (Graddol 1997, 2006).

A central language policy question in the field of science is whether the present day hegemony of one language in the multilingual field of science will give way to the state of monolingual monopoly, just sketched, where English becomes the only allowable language of international and increasingly of national communication, possibly with irreversible consequences for other languages and their communities; or, whether the national and international communities of science will oppose multilingualism being dissolved into monolingualism and opt for plurilingualism as a way to enrich the academic field.

In this paper I briefly sketch the development of language use in international scientific communication, mainly in periodicals, which has led to the dominance of English. I then point out some problems related to language policy decisions that rely solely on language distribution in a small number of international journals, concluding with some caveats and arguments that explore the future dynamics of language use in science.

From Restricted Plurilingualism to the Dominance of English in scientific publications

Whether the normal or typical situation for the field of science was to be dominated by a single language or several in different epochs of history is a matter of debate. Walter (1996) maintains that, throughout the past millennia, there was one language most of the time that was used to articulate sciences in the Occident, from the Sumerian to Greek, Arabic and Latin. Modernity constitutes the exception, when several languages, basically French, English and later on German, gradually substituted Latin. Others (Ehlich 2001) have observed that international monolingual communication has always constituted an idealization which focused on the hegemonic language of its time and the 'invisibilisation' of other languages present in subordinate strands and regions of scientific development. In any case, the period of modernity which founded and vigorously developed modern sciences deployed a system of plurilingualism, albeit limited to a few languages, in the field of science. The 15th century already witnessed a process of popularisation of scientific knowledge in Europe which developed French, English, German, Italian and Russian into scientific languages. Such a course implied a significant societal effort which seems difficult to fully appreciate from today's perspective (Ehlich 2001). From Renaissance to the beginning of Modernity advocates of empirical sciences such as Francis Bacon and the Royal Society in England promoted doing scientific research publicly in the marketplace which meant a democratization of science including the use of the local languages. Furthermore, the great advances of science throughout the Enlightenment in France and elsewhere, namely the extensive public debates, could not have come about without the massive inroads of the national languages in scientific and humanistic endeavours.

At the beginning of the 20th century, three languages, English, French and German, held a central and fairly balanced position in science, although differentiated by disciplines. No one in the developed world could at that time study or do research in medicine, biology or chemistry without reading German and publishing scientific findings in German journals. Similarly, law and political sciences constituted the realm of French, whereas English dominated in political economy and geology (see Ammon 1998 for a detailed account). Throughout the course of the 20th century, however, this balance was lost, not because of intrinsic dynamics in the field of science itself, but due to socio-economic and political factors. The rise of the USA as the dominant economic and political world power since the end of the 19th century, a process accelerated by the two World Wars, constitutes the single most important factor that explains the shift towards English as today's dominant language in international communication including the field of science.

Figure 1 shows the development of language shift between 1880 and 1980, based on publications in American, German, French and Russian bibliographies. Figure 2 gives the continuation of the trends from 1980 to 1996 for the natural sciences, whereas Figure 3 covers the development between 1974 and 1995 for the social sciences. As we can see in Figure 1, English, French and German held a fairly close ranking between 1880 and 1910 when the decline of French began. German, in turn, experienced a significant peak around 1920 when German publications outranked publications in English for a short while. The most important result, however, is the constant rise of English to 64.1% of all publications in 1980, whereas all other languages declined to

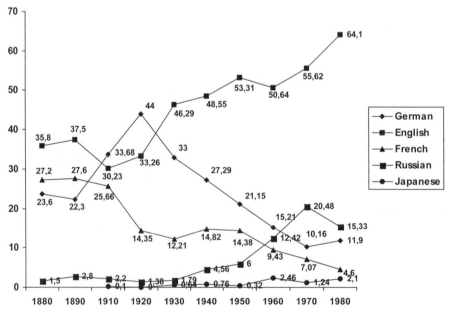

Figure 1. Proportional language use in scientific publications in the course of one century in American, German, French and Russian bibliographies (based on data collected by Tsunoda 1983, in Ammon 1998: 152; Ammon 2006: 3).

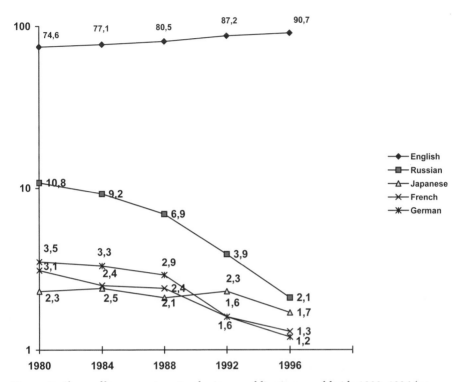

Figure 2. Share of languages in natural science publications worldwide 1880–1996 (per cent of total publications, ordinate compressed; from Ammon, 1998: 152; Ammon 2006: 3).

percentages of between 10 and about 15% for German, and Russian, and to much lower figures for French, Japanese and all other languages. During the time span between 1980 and 1996 that tendency continued. According to Ammon's (1998) figures, English reached a high of 90% for publications in the natural sciences and 82.5% for the social sciences and humanities in the selected periodicals of international ranking by the mid 1990s, with no other language exceeding the 10 per cent mark in this selection of publications.

In the natural sciences English dominance is extreme, and only a few other languages maintain a small percentage of abstracts in international data bases (Table 1). Chemistry seems to be the discipline with a slightly wider language distribution, whereas the "pure" sciences such as mathematics and physics exhibit the highest concentration in English.

Within the social sciences and humanities, although the concentration in English also increases over time, all the languages listed, especially French and German, hold a greater percentage of publications than they do in the natural sciences.

Other sources complete the general picture, as can be seen in two extensive studies produced by the "Centro de Información y Documentación Científica" (Cindoc 1998, 1999) from Spain which evaluated the role of Spanish in scientific publications. Table 3

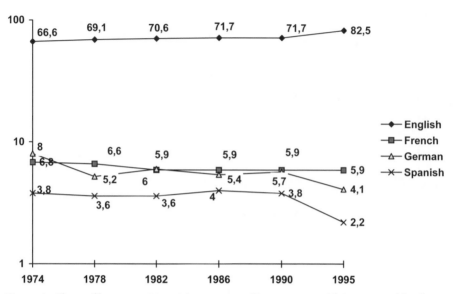

Figure 3. Share of languages in social sciences and humanities publications worldwide 1997–1995 (per cent of total publications, ordinate compressed; from Ammon, 1998: 167; Ammon 2006: 4).

Table 1. Share of languages in several natural sciences in 1996 (sources: Biological, Chemical, Physical Abstracts, Medline, MathSci Disc, adapted from Ammon 1998)

Languages	Biology	Chemistry	Physics	Medicine	Mathematics	Natural Sciences (average)
English	91.6	83.2	94.8	88.6	94.3	90.7
Russian	1.9	3.8	0.2	1.6	3.2	2.1
Japanese	1.1	3.9	1.7	1.8	0.2	1.7
German	1.1	1.9	0.9	2.2	0.3	1.3
French	1.4	0.7	0.4	1.9	2.3	1.2
Chinese	0.8	4.2	1.2	0.1	1.1	–
Spanish	0.6	0.3	0.0	1.2	0.1	–
Italian	0.3	–	0.1	0.6	0.1	–
Portuguese	0.3	–	–	0.1	–	–
Other	0.9	1.1	0.7	1.9	–	3.0

shows the average percentage of publications between 1992 and 1997 in the main languages in relevant data bases for the social sciences and humanities.

Table 2. Share of languages in several social sciences and humanities in 1995 (sources: SocioFile, Historical Abstracts on Disc, The Philosopher's Index, adapted from Ammon 1998)

Languages	Sociology 1996	History 1995	Philosophy 1995	Soc Sc and Hum. 1995
English	85.8	78.0	85.5	82.5
French	4.2	6.0	7.4	5.9
German	4.4	5.3	3.2	4.1
Spanish	1.6	2.8	1.8	2.2
Italian	0.9	2.1	0.8.	–
Japanese	0.2	0.4	0.1	–
Russian	1.5	1.4	–	–
Chinese	–	0.4		–
Other	1.4	3.6	1.2	5.3

Table 3. Share of languages in selected data bases in the social sciences and humanities from 1992 to 1997 (Cindoc 1999).

Data Bases	German	Spanish	French	English	Italian
A & H Search	8.15	2.11	11.65	71.95	3.70
Delphes	0.89	0.90	89.98	7.76	0.49
Econlit	–	1.00	2.20	95.6	1.20
Eric	0.05	0.16	0.37	99.37	0.01
Francis	5.22	4.11	35.02	32.72	4.61
Historical Abstracts	7.85	2.26	6.85	77.73	2.46
LLBA	6.29	1.77	7.82	76.32	1.23
MLA	7.55	6.57	9.02	73.63	2.00
Philosopher Index	7.00	6.33	3.00	78.01	2.66
Psych Info	1.34	0.85	1.16	95.20	0.42
Sociological Abstracts	3.65	2.07	4.56	85.75	1.37
Social Science Search	2.95	0.33	1.64	93.66	0.04

LLBA: Linguistics & Language Behavior Abstracts
MLA: Modern Language Abstracts

Table 4 presents the average percentage of publications in all the consulted sources for the social sciences and humanities for the period of study covered in this research (Cindoc 1999). While in such a short period of time no dramatic changes would be evident, all languages except English and French declined slightly in their percentages[1] with English reaching nearly 75% of all publications by 1997.

Table 4. Average share of languages in all consulted data bases for 1992 to 1997 in per cent (Cindoc 1999)

Languages	1992	1993	1994	1995	1996	1997
English	67.11	68.84	71.50	74.83	71.70	74.57
French	14.02	16.56	16.62	16.81	16.93	16.89
German	4.54	4.59	4.22	4.74	3.77	3.14
Spanish	2.06	2.39	2.27	2.04	2.12	1.37
Italian	1.87	1.73	1.66	1.48	1.56	1.98

The conclusion is that, by the end of the 20th century, English had become the dominant language in selected international journals with 75 per cent or higher of publications. Important differences arise between the natural sciences on the one hand, and the social sciences and humanities on the other with the latter retaining a greater proportion of publications in other languages including in books which continue to play a central role in most social sciences and humanities (Cindoc 1998, 1999). This difference, although small in absolute numbers in this kind of studies, turns out to be relevant for language policies and strategies in the field of science. As a matter of fact, the proportional growth of English masks the absolute growth of publications in many other languages given the rapid expansion of the scientific market in general.

The shift towards English implies that an increasing number of scientists whose mother tongue is not English have shifted to English for publication. An empirical trace of this process can be identified directly in the fact that the number of contributions in English language journals by authors from non Anglophone countries has grown significantly over the past decades. Indirect evidence materializes in the fact that publications in languages such as French, German, Russian or Spanish are increasingly loosing their attraction as places for publication by authors whose mother tongue is not the language of publication. Consequently, the proportion of native authors grows in these publications. This very important process affects the status of international, super central languages which is defined by the fact that participants from outside their native language circle use the language for purposes of international communication. Thus, in terms of Kachru's (1986) framework of three concentric circles that represent the zones of influence of international or imperial languages, the third circle of foreigners using that language is rapidly expanding in the case of English, whereas it is evidently shrinking or even imploding in the case of other super central languages in the field of science. Ammon (1998) provides the following tables (5a and 5b) which show the relative increase of German authors in German language publications, while at the same time their participation in English language publications grows as well.

In sum, when we observe the process of international communication defined narrowly as the exchange of information between speakers of different languages as reflected in a reduced number of high ranking international periodical publications, we can only arrive at the conclusion that relevant scientific findings have to be published in English if their authors want to be acknowledged by the top scientific community

Table 5a. Share of authors from Germany in *Biological Abstracts* (percent of total publications, Ammon 1998: 154).

Biological abstracts	1980	1984	1988	1992	1995
In German-language contributions	22.0	23.6	26.7	10.7	77.2
In English-language contributions	0.7	3.0	3.1	1.4	5.3

Table 5b. Share of authors from Germany in *MathSciDisc* (percent of total publications, Ammon 1998: 154).

MathSciDisc	1975	1980	1982	1983	1985	1990	1995
In German-language contributions	1.3	2.1	4.4	27.7	38.8	51.2	58.0
In English-language contributions	6.0	6.0	6.2	10.2	12.2	12.1	12.3

of their discipline. Even results of utmost relevance and originality, e.g. in natural sciences or medicine, may get lost or pass unnoticed if they are published in any other language.

Monolingualism or plurilingualism in science?

The previous conclusion based on trends in databases calls for further explanation and differentiation. The question whether monolingualism in international scientific communication will finally become the norm and if this is a desirable outcome is a matter of debate.

In many investigations and discussions of language globalisation, and, more broadly, globalisation as such, the past two decades have been characterised by a tendency to not accept the possibility of alternatives to the dominant views, much along the lines of Margaret Thatcher's rude and famous "there is no alternative". For many, therefore, there is no alternative to the English monopoly in international communication. Numerous influential studies, however, exaggerate English dominance, either by using wrong or distorted information[2] or by the very design of their approach and the construction of their data base. Ammon (2003) points out that the databases in the social sciences and humanities he used for his 1998 study are biased towards English and are much less representative for publications worldwide that the ones in the natural sciences. Most biographical databases create a vicious circle of self fulfilling prophecies based on a strong bias in favour of English and Anglophone countries. Such a bias can be inferred from data in the Citation Indexes, as Sandelin and Sarafoglou (2004) pointed out in their study on language and publication statistics. Thus, the Arts and Humanities Citation Index for 2006 cites 62,513 entries in English. Given the selection of journals it happens that Germany, one of the world's leading nations in these fields whose researchers increasingly publish in English, publishes fewer articles in English than Australia and Scotland, Italy ranks behind Wales and Spain behind

New Zealand and Ireland (Table 6). Similarly, in the entries in Spanish for the same year, US contributions are the most frequent (Table 7). If the journals included in these citation indexes were representative of the quality and quantity in a given field, it would mean that the USA outnumbers and produces more noteworthy publications in Spanish than any Spanish-speaking country. Here we find in the selection of journals included not only a significant bias in favour of English as the language of publication, but also in favour of Anglophone countries as the origin of publication in other languages (Baldauf, Jr, and Jernudd 1986). Who selects the journals and who defines the impact factors? Generally speaking, the selected journals create impact through their citation of articles by authors in a self-validating process.

Table 6. Arts & Humanities Citation Index 2006. 62,513 Entries in English by Countries or Territories of Origin

Country	Entries	Country	Entries
USA	18,617	France	356
England	5,776	Wales	335
Canada	1,788	Italy	322
Australia	970	Israel	276
Scotland	792	New Zealand	251
Germany	590	Ireland	209
Netherlands	408	Spain	191

Table 7. Arts & Humanities Citation Index 2006. 1.384 Entries in Spanish by Countries or Territories of Origin

Country	Entries	Country	Entries
USA	245	France	22
Spain	205	Canada	7
Chile	45	England	6
Argentina	28	Italy	6
Mexico	27	Peru	5

The focus on English blurs our view of the existence of important and well-established circles of international academic communication outside English such as the international networks of the Francophonie which comprises over 50 countries and their universities (*Association des Universités francophones, AUF*). Every year ACFAS, the *Association Francophone pour le Savoir*, organises a large congress in Québec with several thousand papers in all fields of science that are presented overwhelmingly in French, even by participants from Anglophone countries. Certainly, French is the most visible case of status loss as international language which includes the field of science. However, international studies on the topic hardly ever acknowledge the close networks and intensive international communication in science that functions in French (Rousseau 2005).

Similarly, Hispanic America and Spain maintain solid and massive academic communication in Spanish which is more autonomous in the social sciences and humanities than in the natural sciences. This network comprises many thousands of journals published mostly in Spanish. UNAM, the leading Mexican university with over 300,000 students, created *Latindex*, a scientific index which includes 11,000 periodical publications from Latin America, the Caribbean, Spain and Portugal, out of which 2,883 are Brazilian (Café 2005).

Over the past decade, the linguistic and academic integration of Brazil, which produces 40 per cent of Latin America's scientific publications (Café 2005), with its main Hispanophone neighbours, has progressed significantly through the Common Market of the Southern Cone (Mercosur). General communication including academic exchange and cooperation are based on a language policy of receptive bilingualism in Spanish and Portuguese, with no need to revert to English (Hamel 2003b). Few experts would expect that Brazil alone produces 5,986 scientific and technical journals (Instituto Brasileiro de Informação em Ciência e Tecnologia, in Café 2005). The overwhelming majority of them are published in Portuguese, but only 17 are registered in the international Science Citation Index (Café 2005).[3] Who reads these journals, what do they publish, and why would their circulation not be of relevance according to standards exclusively defined by the increasingly monolingual Anglophone academia and their satellites in other language areas?

The previous discussion posits the question about what we understand by <u>international</u> scientific communication, how it relates to other scientific communication and to what extent it makes sense to separate scientific communication (publications and conference presentations) from the whole process of scientific production. International communication sould not be reduced to interlingual communication, i. e. the interaction between speakers of different language communities, but should include the extensive and diverse scientific communication of established networks inside Francophonie, the Luso-Hispanic or the Anglophone world.

Furthermore, the dynamics of scientific communication seem to signal a tendency of internationalisation which makes it more and more difficult to distinguish between national and international communication. I would argue that globalisation is increasingly diluting the distinction between the national and the international sphere, and is dissolving nation-states altogether (Hardt and Negri 2000) — with the exception of the USA. As it happens, the thrust for English as the only world language in science blurs the hegemony of a single national state, the USA, under the label of 'globalisation' and creates the ideology that English has already become so international that it neither belongs to any country, nor is it controlled by any group of native speakers (Crystal 1997, see a critique in Hamel 2006b). Authors critical of this stance belonging to super central language communities such as French and German (Durand 2001, 2006, Ehlich 2001, 2005) have identified traces of cultural imperialism in this process which not only affects the national scientific cultures but the development of science as a whole. The US scientific market is largely organised in terms of a national and imperial structure which admits subordinate foreign participation within the frameworks established by US science, but not as a global market. Its impressive capacity to individually shape and absorb foreign scientific intelligentsia and thus maintain its worldwide lead does not suggest that there is any significant influence of other scientific communities in its structure or organisation. The same applies to language use where tolerance of foreign pronunciation of English only superficially covers up the real language and discourse requirements for academic work in English only.

On the other hand, the national scientific organisation of the world's most powerful country significantly influences the course and structure of science policies in most other countries. Therefore, while the idea of introducing a kind of diglossic barrier between international scientific communication in English and national communication in the local languages that could shelter the latter looks quite attractive at first sight (e. g. Ammon 2006), this is less feasible in a globalising world since linguistic boundaries coincide less and less with national borders, as is highlighted in the debate on language use in science in the Scandinavian countries (Phillipson 2001, 2003) or in the European Union (Ammon and McConnell 2002). What we witness is in fact a process of increasing linguistic hierarchisation and of domain loss for lower ranking languages. Stable language boundaries tend to disappear. Once English is declared the only international language for science, all other languages not only lose international status but are menaced in their own territories, as Durand (2001, 2006) stringently argues.

Similarly, the linguistic and conceptual division operated in many studies between the communication of results and the larger field it belongs to, i.e. the field of scientific production, circulation, and the construction of human capital through academic teaching and team-working, becomes arguable when submitted to closer scrutiny. Congress papers and publications are integrated into the larger cycle of scientific production which is by itself a communicative social process that implies a research community. The attempt to isolate the external communication part and assign a language to it that differs from the one used in the rest of the process may only transfer linguistic and other conceptual conflicts from one place to another in the field of science. In any case, integrated plurilingual models in the whole field of science are called for to attend possible conflicts (Hamel 2006a).

Ultimately, the difficulties of introducing clear-cut diglossic barriers in any part of the process of producing, teaching and diffusing science has deep roots in the very nature of the science-and-language relation, i.e. in the language of science itself. The idea of an abstract language structure common to all languages whose slots only need to be filled with interchangeable technical terminology from each language may have risen within natural sciences where the very process of acquiring scientific knowledge is largely identified with memorising technical nomenclature, at least in the beginning (e. g. in medicine). Scientific language, however, is much more than that, especially if we focus on the *alltägliche Wissenschaftssprache*, the everyday language of science, as Ehlich (2001: 7) calls it. Beyond the specific scientific terminology, this register uses a particular national language with its structure and idiomatic properties for the purposes of oral and written communication. Consequently, we can only access world scientific knowledge through the existing languages and their structures, which provides a perspective of diversity to the dynamics of world knowledge development (Ehlich 2001). The experience of multiple perspectives enshrined in specific languages of science may constitute a relevant barrier against scientific ethnocentrism often disguised under the cover of globalism.

Beyond the individual experiences, it has been argued that the reduction of science to one language could severely hamper the development of science itself. This line of thought is related to Humboldt's and Herder's view of the role languages play for cultures and nations, and to the Sapir-Whorf hypothesis about cultural relativism and linguistic determinism, a debate that has been referred to in many publications on the topic of language and science (e.g. Ammon 2006, Durand 2001, Ehlich 2001). More important than to discuss whether research findings formulated in one language can be properly translated into another is to acknowledge the risks and the possibility of distorted results that may derive from the study of language use in science based on a narrow concept of language as an abstract structural entity, and to exclude from the analysis its interrelation with power relations, discourse structures and cultural models underlying research orientations (Hamel 2003a). A comprehensive investigation, that includes these three components would have to show to what extent the present process of spreading English in science implies the imposition of a specific Anglo-Saxon scientific discourse and related cultural models, research paradigms and selection of topics. Power relations and hierarchisation of prestige between approaches, scientific schools, disciplines and lobby groups from outside turn out to play a fundamental role in the dynamics of science, as Bourdieu (1984) so masterly demonstrated when analysing *Academia* as a sociological field. The new hierarchy with English on top, including its discourse structures and related cultural models, constitutes a powerful instrument and at the same time an outcome of this broader process.

The increasing supremacy of English reinforces a tendency towards growing monolingualism in science. Whereas only fifty or seventy years ago Anglophone scientists could hardly afford to ignore relevant literature in at least a few other languages, today they can deny the very existence of scientific results outside English and re-invent the wheel as is often ironically observed from outside. On the one hand, this process generates bi- or multilingual language proficiency among non Anglophones. An important argument in favour of scientific monolingualism has always been the fact that non-Anglophones, especially speakers of languages which are marginal to science, would only have to learn one foreign language instead of several, an argument that cannot be easily dismissed (Ammon 2006).

On the other hand, it reinforces a tendency towards individual and societal monolingualism among Anglophones who feel less and less inclined to acquire foreign languages for science and other purposes of international communication when they can achieve their goals and do their business in English. Such an individual and societal language policy is based on the rationale that, to learn any or even several foreign languages for academic purposes would not provide the Anglophone academic with an access to more bibliography than English alone can supply, as Ammon (2006) correctly points out. Furthermore, it saves the Anglophone countries and their speakers a significant investment in capital, effort and time by not learning other languages (Grin 2005). Another perhaps more profound reason for such an "English only" strategy is the perpetuation of an asymmetric power relation between the Anglophone native speakers and their non native counterparts in international communication. Many of our Anglophone colleagues in the fields of second language acquisition, bilingual education or multilingualism celebrate linguistic diversity in theory but practice functional monolingualism since they do not publish, teach or communicate in any other language. In English they can play their role as communicative stars at international conferences or promote their publications that are usually better formulated, without having to be more sound or profound than those of the non native authors. Such individual and societal strategies may provide advantages in the short term. It bars the monolingual researchers, however, from acquiring the fundamental experience of encountering multiple research perspectives through knowledge framed in other languages, and to measure their own knowledge against the possible world knowledge formulated in a diversity of languages. Beyond such personal experience, individual and societal monolingualism is regarded increasingly as a handicap in a modern, globalising world, both by representatives of the English language industry that profits from the expansion of English (Crystal 1997; Graddol 1997, 2006) and by those who oppose scientific and other types of monolingualism (Durand 2001, 2006; Ehlich 2001, Hamel 2005, 2006a; Phillipson 2003).

The dominance of English in science and its perspectives

The present pre-eminence of English language use in scientific publications has already severely reduced multilingualism in the field, and may eliminate the status of any other language as an international language of science. Figures and forecasts send out a mixed message for future development. Most of them seem to suggest that there is an inevitable course of affairs towards an English monopoly. This is furthermore presented as a natural process and by-product of globalisation by many experts. If you want to have your research findings read by the relevant international scientific community, so the story goes, you have to publish in English. Whether this tendency is desirable or not is a matter of international and national debate where many actors understandably take sides according to the perceived interests of their professional and language communities.

As we have seen, many investigations on the use of languages in science reduce their object of study step by step to focus on the language of publication in a small, selected number of prestigious international journals included in the main databases and citation indexes that today are predominantly published by English language enterprises. Certainly, journals well documented in large databases are fairly easy to research for language use, compared to the complex sociolinguistic field of production, circulation and diffusion of science. Thus, this strand of research usually isolates scientific communication, mainly its publications, from the field of science as a whole with its possible negative consequences. Finally, the complex relation between languages, discourse structures and cultural models is not examined and the fundamental question to what extent dominant research paradigms and their ideological construction profit from the integration of the these three components but spread even beyond language borders is not pursued, with rare exceptions.

In the previous section I have argued why such systematic reductions in the construction of language use in science as an object of research may be tainted with liguicentrism and objectively trigger off a circle of self fulfilling prophecies. Given such reductions in the scope of research, it should not be surprising that overwhelmingly the figures and the supposedly inevitable arguments for natural processes pave the way to English monolingualism.

Any language policy proposals will have to tackle the complex question whether stable language domains can be established that recognise English as the sole international language of science and find some niches for other languages, mainly on the intra-national level and for academic teaching (e.g. Ammon 2006, Ammon and McConnell 2002). Interestingly, the Francophonie discussed this question over 20 years ago, namely whether the whole field of the natural sciences was already 'lost' for French and should be abandoned to English (see Walter 1996 and Maurais' personal communication in 2003). Such a position was however never adopted by French institutions. Durand (2001, 2006), a firm defender of French *and* plurilinguism in science, strongly argues against the recognition of English or any other language as the sole international language of science, since that would entail negative consequences not only for French but for the role of French scientific contributions as a whole. Contrary to a common view he argues that, if French scientific findings were exclusively published in English, French science would lose visibility and recognition on the international scene. Such a policy would furthermore deter people around the globe from learning French or any other language except English.

I have elsewhere (Hamel 2003a, 2005, 2006a) argued in favour of a plurilingual enrichment model for Spanish as a language of science that might help to avoid a zero sum game and the "either — or" dichotomy present in approaches that assume the unrestricted defense of a given language and foster monolingualism. Plurilingualism entails a view of intercultural communication where ones own position or academic standpoint recognises that other perspectives and procedures are also part of the possible world knowledge; or, to put it another way, that other valid positions and knowledge bases exist that may be formulated in terms of different languages, discourse structures and cultural model that define research paradigms.

Ammon (2006: 19) proposes an interesting scheme of hypothetic attitudes that inform and guide linguistic behaviour among academics and determine reading preferences. First, he establishes a reading preference hierarchy between English, other international languages and non international languages which is probably irrefutable based on sheer language competence and numbers of publications. More interestingly, he postulates that both Anglophones and non Anglophones prefer to read texts written by Anglophone native speakers over those written by non native language users who publish in English. Such a predilection, if it turned out to be empirically sustained, would have to be explained, not so much in terms of stylistic quality, but rather in terms of discourse structures and cultural models that correspond to dominant research paradigms. Readers — academics or others — enjoy texts that confirm their own knowledge, beliefs and values including familiar ways of organising texts. Beyond that basic preference, critical readers probably rather look for contributions from other cultural and linguistic communities to whose languages they have no direct access. Furthermore, those researchers who keep track of publications in a number languages have certainly experienced that, while fundamental contributions appear in leading English language journals, there is also a huge amount of low quality work being published in English, given the sheer numbers of publications and the economic interests of publishing houses. Very often native writers of English find it easier than non natives to have their work published, even if their contribution adds little to the field, just because they are capable of formulating their papers in mainstream conventional discourse styles. Conversely, we often hit upon real jewels of inspiring research formulated in other languages that are fully integrated into the sophisticated research traditions of, say, French, German or Spanish social and philosophical thought that may never reach the English language market or appear only years later.

Ammon's typology should therefore be broadened by adding some alternative attitudes that characterise the critical researcher oriented towards plurilingualism:

1. To actively read scientific literature in as many languages as possible.
2. To prefer texts in their original languages over translations.
3. To quote the original texts — with translation only if necessary — to counteract the growing 'invisibilisation' of other languages than English in scientific texts.
4. To avoid the translation of titles into English in reference lists.
5. To present whenever possible one's own papers in the host country's language.

The perspectives of the future constellations of language relations seem to be largely uncertain in a rapidly changing world. In 1997, Graddol (1997: 58) argued that in the course of the 21st century no single language would occupy the monopolistic position which English achieved by the end of the 20th century. Rather, an array of some six languages would form an oligopoly as the world's dominant languages. In his updated prognosis on the future of world languages, Graddol (2006) moves English from the role of a foreign language to that of a basic skill comparable to computer skills for almost any society. But he argues forcefully that "English will not be enough" in the UK, the USA or elsewhere (Graddol 2006: 118–119) to survive in a future multilingual world society. The same in my view applies to the field of science: "English will not be enough", neither to enhance international communication in science nor to foster creativity and diversity in the scientific research of the future.

Many experts had identified the rise of the USA as the dominant economic, political and military power since the end of the 19th century as the single most important factor to explain the hegemony of English. If in the soon future a monopolar power relation that existed since the end of the Cold War will give way to a multipolar world which revitalises the role of Europe and includes the BRIC states as emerging superpowers, there is no reason to take the survival of English as the only world language for granted, even if it is increasingly taking on the status of world *lingua franca* that has autonomy from its internal circle (Kachru 1986) of native speaking countries. Those who reject other languages and attempt to formalise a language policy that institutionalises English as the only international language of science already may be outdated, caught in a phase of globalisation and an ideal of monolingual communication that is coming to an end. In light of this it can be argued that those language communities that preserve the vitality, updating and presence of their languages in the field of science, even if they occupy only a small percentage in international publications, provide an important service for their own language community and the international community of science. They avoid possibly irreversible language attrition for their own languages and contribute to maintaining a plurilingual perspective in the field of science. Maybe such a plural language policy will help to open the *AILA Review* again to languages other than English, and we may see articles published in Spanish, Chinese, Arabic or Hindi at some point in the future.

Notes

1. in Table 3 and 4, the numbers for French are significantly distorted, i. e. they range much higher than in other comparisons due to the inclusion of the French Delphis data base which assigns over 70% of its coverage to French publications.

2. According to Graddol (1997: 11), 19 countries that are currently shifting from an EFL status (English as a foreign language) to a L2 status for English, meaning that "the use of English for intranational use is greatly increasing". At least for Argentina, Honduras and Nicaragua that are among the countries he mentions such an assertion is clearly wrong. Later on Graddol (2006) acknowledges that the very distinction of L2 status is losing its meaning, and, following Kachru (2004), he suggests that different levels of proficiency among learners should rather be considered when analysing the role of English. However, the massive distribution of his oeuvre has left the wrong impression that Latin America is shifting to English in a way comparable to many Asian countries. This is certainly not the case.

3. To render Brazilian research and Portuguese more visible in international science, the Brazilian federal government created an online library (SCIELO, Scientific Electronic Library Online) with 92 selected Brazilian journals, mainly in the field of medicine. 16.3 % of them publish only in English, but almost a third (32.6%) accept articles in English, Portuguese of Spanish, the three languages usually read by Brazilian scientists (Café 2005).

References

Ammon, U. 1998. *Ist Deutsch noch internationale Wissenschaftssprache? Englisch auch für die Lehre an den deutschsprachigen Hochschulen.* Berlin: de Gruyter.

Ammon, U. 2003. Global English and the non-native speaker: Overcoming disadvantage. In *Language in the Twenty-First Century*, H. Tonkin & T. Reagan (eds), 23–34. Amsterdam: John Benjamins.

Ammon, U. 2006. Language planning for international scientific communication: An overview of questions and potential solutions. *Current Issues in Language Planning* 7(1): 1–30.

Ammon, U. & McConnell, G. 2002. *English as an Academic Language in Europe.* Frankfurt: Peter Lang.

Baldauf Jr., R.B. & Jernudd, B. H. 1986. Aspects of language use in cross-cultural psychology. *Australian Journal of Psychology* 32(3): 381–392.

Bourdieu, P. 1984. *Homo academicus.* Paris: Minuit.

Café, L. 2005. A língua portuguesa nas publicações científicas: O caso brasileiro. In *Congreso Internacional sobre Lenguas Neolatinas en la Comunicación Especializada*, Centro de Estudios Lingüísticos y Literarios (ed.), 141–147. México: Agence Intergouvernamentale de la Francophonie, El Colegio de México, Unión Latina.

Cindoc (Centro de Información y Documentación Científica). 1998. La producción científica en español. In *Anuario Instituto Cervantes.* Madrid. http://cvc.cervantes.es/obref/anuario/anuario_98.

Cindoc (Centro de Información y Documentación Científica). 1999. El español en las revistas de ciencia y tecnología recogidas en ocho bases de datos internacionales. In *Anuario Instituto Cervantes*, Madrid. http://cvc.cervantes.es/obref/anuario/anuario_99.

Crystal, D. 1997. *English as a Global Language.* Cambridge: CUP.

De Swaan, A. 1993. The emergent world language system: An introduction. *International Political Science Review* 14(3): 219–26.

De Swaan, A. 2001. *Words of the World. The Global Language System.* Cambridge: Polity Press.

Durand, C. 2001. *La mise en place des monopoles du savoir.* Paris: L'Harmattan.

Durand, C. 2006. If it's not in English, it's not worth reading!. *Current Issues in Language Planning* 7(1): 44–60.

Ehlich, K. 2001. Wissenschaftssprachkomparatistik. In *Mehrsprachige Wissenschaft — europäische Perspektiven. Eine Konferenz im Europäischen Jahr der Sprachen*, K. Ehlich (ed.), 1–10. München: Universität München.

Ehlich, K. 2005. Deutsch als Medium wissenschaftlichen Arbeitens. In *Englisch oder Deutsch in internationalen Studiengängen?*, M. Motz (ed.), 41–51. Frankfurt: PeterLang.

Graddol, D. 1997. *The Future of English?* London: The British Council.

Graddol, D. 2006. *English Next. Why global English may mean the end of 'English as a foreign language'.* London: The British Council.

Grin, F. 2005. L'enseignement des langues étrangères comme politique publique. Rapport établi à la demande du Haut Conseil de l'Évaluation de l'École. Paris : Haut Conseil de l'Évaluation de l'École.

Hamel, R.E. 2003a. El español como lengua de las ciencias frente a la globalización del inglés. Diagnóstico y propuestas de acción para una política latinoamericana del lenguaje en el campo de las ciencias y la educación superior. México DF: UAM.

Hamel, R.E. 2003b. Regional blocs as a barrier against English hegemony? The language policy of Mercosur in South America. In *Languages in a Globalising World*, J. Maurais & M.A. Morris (eds.), 111–142. Cambridge: CUP.

Hamel, R.E. 2005. El español en el campo de las ciencias: propuestas para una política del lenguaje. In *Congreso Internacional sobre Lenguas Neolatinas en la Comunicación Especializada* Centro de Estudios Lingüísticos y Literarios (ed.), 87–112. México: Agence Intergouvernamentale de la Francophonie, El Colegio de México, Unión Latina.

Hamel, R.E. 2006a. Spanish in science and higher education: perspectives for a plurilingual language policy in the Spanish speaking world. *Current Issues in Language Planning* 7(1): 95–125.

Hamel, R.E. 2006b. The development of language empires. In *Sociolinguistics — Soziolinguistik. An international handbook of the science of language and society*, U. Ammon, N. Dittmar, K.J. Mattheier & P. Trudgill, (eds.), Volume 3, 2240–2258. Berlin: Walter de Gruyter,

Hardt, M. & Negri, A. 2000. *Empire*. Cambridge MA: Harvard University Press.

Kachru, B.1986. *The Alchemy of English: The spread, functions and models of non-native Englishes*. Oxford: Pergamon.

Kachru, B. 2004. *Asian Englishes: Beyond the canon*. Hong Kong: Hong Kong University Press.

Kaplan, R.B. 2001. English — the accidental language of science. In *The Dominance of English as a Language of Science — Effects on Other Languages and Language Communities*, U. Ammon (ed.), 3–26. Berlin: Mouton de Gruyter.

Phillipson, R. 1992. *Linguistic Imperialism*. Oxford: OUP.

Phillipson, R. 2001. English or no to English in Scandinavia? *English Today* 17(2): 22–28.

Phillipson, R. 2003. *English-Only Europe?* London: Routledge

Rousseau, L.J. 2005. Le français dans la communication scientifique et technique. In *Congreso Internacional sobre Lenguas Neolatinas en la Comunicación Especializada*, Centro de Estudios Lingüísticos y Literarios (ed.), 113–140. México: Agence Intergouvernamentale de la Francophonie, El Colegio de México, Unión Latina.

Sandelin, B. & Sarafoglou, N. 2004. Language and scientific publication statistics. *Language Problems and Language Planning* 28(1): 1–10.

Skutnabb-Kangas, T. 2004. Políticas del lenguaje y educación: el papel de la educación en la destrucción o el soporte de la diversidad lingüística. *Dimensión Antropológica* 10(28): 91–186. (English version http://www.linguapax.org/congres/plenaries/skutnabb.html).

Tsunoda, M. 1983. Les langues internationales dans les publications scientifiques et techniques. *Sophia Linguistica* 13: 144–155.

Walter, H. 1996. L'évolution des langues de la communication scientifique. Le français et les langue scientifiques de demain ». *Congrès de l'Association francophone pour le savoir (ACFAS)* 1996, Montréal, http://www.acfas.ca/evenements/conf_inaugurale.html.

Author's address

R. E. Hamel
Antiguo Camino a San Pedro Mártir 42–3
14630 México, D. F.
Mexico

ehamel@xanum.uam.mx

Tackling the Anglophones' free ride

Fair linguistic cooperation with a global lingua franca

Philippe Van Parijs

Université catholique de Louvain, Belgium

In science and in all other domains that require communication across borders, we need one lingua franca, and this lingua franca will be English. The adoption of the native language of some as everyone's lingua franca unavoidably raises a problem of justice in various senses. One of these is cooperative justice, the fair distribution of the cost of producing a public good. This article proposes a criterion of fair burden sharing — proportionality of cost to benefit — and explores its policy implications.

Does this criterion require a linguistic tax on the native speakers of the lingua franca in order to subsidize the learning of it by all others? If so, how high should the subsidy be, and should it be pitched at the same per capita level for all learning communities? If not, is there an alternative way of implementing a fair compensation for the free riding of lingua franca natives on everyone else's learning?

Among the article's conclusions are that fair subsidies would need to be directed disproportionately to the Chinese — even abstracting from possible differences in the difficulty of learning English — and that more hopes should be focused on the compensatory poaching of the web than on anything resembling a linguistic tax.

Introduction

Let us not beat around the bush. In science and in all other domains which require communication across borders, we need a lingua franca. One lingua franca. As quickly as possible. And this lingua franca will be English.

Is this a problem? Yes it is. Not because it needs to entail Anglo-American ideological hegemony: it is up to all of us non-Anglophones to grab the megaphone and use English to say whatever we wish to say, instead of whispering our clever thoughts — and our frustration — in our (henceforth) provincial tongues. But the adoption of

AILA Review 20 (2007), 72–86. DOI 10.1075/aila.20.07van
ISSN 1461–0213 / E-ISSN 1570–5595 © John Benjamins Publishing Company

the native language of some as everyone's lingua franca unavoidably raises a problem of justice in three distinct senses.

1.   Fair cooperation as proportionality between benefit and cost

Firstly, a common language can be viewed as a public good, and linguistic justice can then be understood as fair cooperation. Secondly, one's linguistic competence can be viewed as a personal asset, and linguistic justice can then be conceived as equality of opportunities. And thirdly, one's native language can be viewed as a core component of one's collective identity, and linguistic justice can then be conceived as equality of dignity. I shall restrict myself here to the first of these three interpretations, cooperative justice.[1] As a point of departure, I shall briefly present without argument the criterion of fair burden sharing which I believe best captures the demands of linguistic justice in this first sense, and then concentrate on the policy implications. Both the principle and the implications are meant to apply across the board, in all domains in which a lingua franca is emerging. But the possess, as we shall see, special relevance to scientific communication.

In the first of our three interpretations, then, a common language is viewed as a public good, and linguistic injustice is understood as free riding by some on the learning effort made by others. A common language benefits all the people it enables to communicate with one another. But if the language serving this function is the native tongue of some of these people a subset of the population benefits without contributing itself to the production of the public good.

The criterion I propose (and defend elsewhere) as a general criterion of fair cooperation requires that one should equalise the ratio of (gross) benefit to cost for everyone involved or, put differently, that every cooperator should benefit from the public good proportionally to the cost he or she incurred by contributing to its production.[2] The benefit is here most conveniently understood as the gross gain from cooperation, i.e. the gain abstracting from any cost incurred. But if gross benefit is proportional to cost, so is net benefit. And the criterion therefore amounts to requiring the cooperative surplus to be distributed in proportion to each party's contribution to the cost of producing it. Since the learning is only worth doing if the total (gross) benefit exceeds the total (gross) cost, the ratio of total benefit to total cost must be strictly larger than 1. What the proposed criterion requires is that this overall ratio should apply to each speaker involved, and hence also to each of the two communities taken as a whole.

As a rough and simple approximation, suppose the gross benefit of one person learning a language known by others is measured by the sum of numbers of speech partners that are thereby gained by the various people involved. If one unilingual A-native learns language B spoken by n unilingual B-speakers, the gross benefit is then n for each B-learning A-native speaker and n too for the B-native linguistic community whenever one A-native learns B. Under this simple assumption, the gross benefit is therefore equal for both communities, but the cost is borne by just one of them. Co-operative justice as proportionality between cost and benefit requires that this cost should also be equal, and hence — prima facie — that the community whose language is being learned should subsidize the community which is doing the learning up to the point where the cost, somehow measured, become equal. In other words, fairness requires, under the assumptions made, a fifty-fifty sharing of the cost between lingua franca natives and lingua franca learners. This is the basic ethical intuition the real-world implications of which we are now going to explore.

2.   A fifty-fifty contribution by the Anglo countries?

Whether coerced or spontaneous, asymmetric bilingualism has been a frequent phe-nomenon in many places for a long time. But as schooling, mobility and communica-tion expand and intensify, it is becoming more ubiquitous and more massive than ever, with English strengthening from one day to the next its position as a worldwide lingua franca. This ubiquitous asymmetric bilingualism is undoubtedly very efficient but, by the standards of our proposed criterion, it is also very unfair. To make it fair, transfers are required. Can one make some intelligent guesses as to how high they would need to be?

One possible point of departure is the average time required to master adequately a non-native natural language. One guess is 10.000 hours — compared to a standard school year totalling less than 1.000 hours in the classroom (Piron 2001: 95). But this sort of estimate is pretty tricky. In the first place, the notion of "mastering" a foreign language is extremely fuzzy. Once the basic syntax and morphology are learned, hun-dreds of hours may be needed for tiny improvements in pronunciation, fluency, use of idiomatic expressions and respect of grammatical exceptions, as well as for expanding one's lexical repertoire. At what stage should the timer be stopped? Secondly, the num-ber of hours required through a classroom method for any given level of competence is highly dependent on linguistic distance between one's mother tongue (and other languages previously learned) and the language to be learned. Should only some com-binations of languages be considered, and how should they be weighed to provide an average? Thirdly and most importantly, the effectiveness of what happens inside the classroom is crucially dependent on motivation and opportunity and hence on what is going on outside the classroom. The "average" time needed to achieve any level of pro-ficiency in a language is therefore crucially dependent on the way in which the various combinations of native language background, language to be learned and context are weighted — a rather tricky matter, both conceptually and empirically, to put it mildly.

A more relevant and reliable point of departure can be sought in estimates of the cost of actual language learning. Here again, pitfalls abound. But a reasonable conjec-ture has been made on the basis of the difference between the annual per capita cost of language teaching in state schools in France and in the United Kingdom: €100.[3]

There are various factors that bias this estimate upward and above all downward. In particular, it does not incorporate the cost of private tuition nor the opportunity cost (for both teachers and learners) of language learning. But let us adopt this as a conservative estimate. How much can the Brits expect to pay? How much can the French hope to receive?

Suppose first that the world reduces to the French and British populations (of about equal sizes), each supposed to be linguistically homogeneous, and hence that the learning of English by the French serves no other purpose than to enable the two populations to communicate, actively and passively, with one another. Suppose also that the benefits of this learning are enjoyed symmetrically by both sides. Here again there are biases in both directions. On the one hand, the Brits are able to talk, bargain, argue, etc. with the French with the advantage of using a language in which they feel more comfortable. On the other hand, language learning provides the French with an access to English-language material accumulated through the centuries, and such access is of little benefit to contemporary Brits. Assuming equal levels of benefit may therefore be reasonable enough. Under these assumptions, our criterion implies that half the cost of €100 per capita should be billed to the British government, and hence €50 per capita or roughly three billion euros transferred annually as a fair contribution to the current learning of English by the French.

However, the Brits and the French are not alone on the planet. Very roughly again, there are five times more English natives than there are people living in the UK, and one hundred times more non-English natives than there are people living in France. Assuming, for simplicity's sake, that the level and cost of learning of English is the same in the rest of the non-Anglo world as in France, the total cost is multiplied by one hundred, and hence also the part of it to be funded by the Anglo countries, now up to 300 billion euros. Fortunately for the UK, this amount is to be shared with other Anglo countries. But unfortunately for all of them, this makes only five times more people, and the per capita subsidy they owe to the rest of the world, it seems, is therefore multiplied by twenty — up to €1000 per capita.

3.   A cheaper deal? Non-natives talking to non-natives

Is this right? No, it is not. It would only be right if the lingua franca learners consisted of one big community of 6 billion people who already share the same native language, and hence for whom the benefit of learning English reduces to communication with the Anglophones. But the six billion non-Anglophones are split up among six thousand distinct native languages, and even for the many among them who know a non-native language other than English that enables them to communicate with some of the others, access to English is also a major potential benefit to them by virtue of the many non-Anglophones with which convergence on English enables them to communicate. Because of this huge additional benefit accruing to English learners, achieving proportionality between cost and benefit can be expected to require a smaller transfer from English natives to English learners. How much smaller?

Here is a simple and rough arithmetic exercise that will enable us to get an order of magnitude. Suppose that the non-Anglo population of the world consists of 100 linguistic groups of 60 million speakers, 10% of which are competent in English. The benefit conferred by competence in English to each of the six million speakers of each language who have learned it is then given by the number of Anglo natives (300 Mn) plus the six million English learners in each of the other non Anglo communities (99 × 6 Mn). The aggregate benefit to the Anglo population is then no longer 50% of the total benefit, but about 25%. (See Appendix 1 for details.) Suppose that we extrapolate the expenditure estimate for France and that the 10% rate of competence in English in each of the 100 non-Anglo communities is achieved at an average cost of €100 per capita (relative to the total population, not the part of it that is proficient in English). The total learning bill is then 600 billion euros (100 × 60 Mn × 100), but only a quarter of it, not a half, needs to be funded out of Anglo pockets. This amounts to €500 (=(60 Bn/300 Mn) × 0.25) per capita for the 300 million Anglophones, rather than the €1000 conjectured above, and hence to a per capita subsidy to the non-Anglophone communities of €25 (= €500 × 300Mn/6Bn), i.e. one quarter of their cost.

Should the share to be borne by the Anglophones not be expected to decrease further as more and more people learn English in all other linguistic communities and hence benefit more and more from each other's learning? This is correct. Under the assumptions made about the number and sizes of the linguistic groups, the Anglo community would only be liable to about 5% of the cost if everyone learned. (See Appendix 2 for details.) But at the same time, the total cost of learning would of course increase tenfold, as the number of learners rises from 10% to 100% of each of the non-Anglo communities. Hence, as a rough estimate of the long-term prospect for the Anglo community of the fair cost of its language having become universal, we are back to a contribution of €1000 (= (100 × 60 Mn × 100 × 10/ 300 Mn) × 0.05. The average subsidy received by each member of a learning community can then be calculated by dividing the total Anglo contribution by the non-Anglo population. This yields €50 (= €1000 × 300/6000), equal to the amount received by the French in our initial two-country scenario, but now covering 5% instead of 50% of the total learning cost.

Our illustrations so far have supposed that the learning communities are of equal sizes. But size inequality not only justifies different levels of aggregate and per capita subsidy (both increasing with size), but may even justify transfers from smaller to larger communities (de Briey & Van Parijs 2002). The subsidy to the learning by large communities would then be co-funded by the Anglo community and small non-Anglo communities. Given the distribution of potential learners among linguistic communities in our real world, however, this latter situation is unlikely to arise. Subsidies could only be required from small learning communities if the biggest learning community — the Mandarinophones — were much bigger, relative to the others, than it already is (see Appendix 1). But differences in size do lead to differences in subsidy levels.

Again some simple arithmetic exercises can give an idea of the orders of magnitude. With a level of learning that makes 10% of the non-Anglo communities proficient in English and costs them €100 per capita, the subsidy amounts to €32 per capita for a community of 1 billion Chinese, and to slightly over and slightly under €24 per capita, respectively, for communities of 60 million French speakers and 4 million Danes, while tax on the Anglo population amounts to over €500 per capita. With a level of learning that reaches 100% of the population and costs €1000 per capita, the per capita subsidy would jump to over €170 for the Chinese, stagnate around €25 for the French and fall to below €17 for the Danes, while the per capita tax on the Anglos would rise to €937. (See Appendix 3 for details.) Even the Chinese, who pocket 60% of the total subsidy, are compensated for only a fraction of the cost of learning (17%), basically because the bulk of the reward of learning English now comes from speaking it with non-natives.

4.   A cheaper deal? Shrinking the cost

Many simplifications were needed above to get some useful orders of magnitude. One of them is that the cost of learning English is the same for everyone and constant over time. Obviously, the cost of learning a completely alien language — as English is for the Chinese — can be expected to greatly exceed, for any indicator of oral or written proficiency, the cost of learning what is just a variant of one's own — as English is for the French. Taking this complication into account would require fairness to boost the overall level of subsidy (at the expense of English natives, who would be better off with more French and less Chinese in the world) and to direct a greater proportion of it to non-indo-European populations (the French would lose, the Chinese would gain).

However, how much a difference it makes depends on the learning method used. The schoolish learning of grammar and vocabulary by adults may both involve a big difference between costs depending on the native language of the learner and cost a lot more, for a given level of proficiency, than immersion, media exposure and other interactive methods at a young age. What must be used as the basis for calculating the Anglo community's fair liability — and everyone else's fair entitlement — is arguably not the actual cost incurred, however sloppy the learning method used, but rather the most efficient of the methods to which the community can reasonably be assumed to have access. By dubbing films, or voicing them over, instead of subtitling them, some linguistic communities foolishly deprive themselves of very effective tools used by others. Both fairness and efficiency recommend that they should not be compensated for these wasteful choices. Whether through increased contributions (from the non-learners) or reduced subsidies (for the learners), other linguistic communities cannot be expected to foot any portion of the resulting extra bill.

Another factor of the learning cost is endogenous to the very diffusion of the lingua franca. As competence in English spreads worldwide, the quantity of learning may be rising, but its unit cost is bound to fall for two reasons. First, both the general and the local spread of competence in English make it possible to provide prospective learners far more cheaply with the competent teachers they need: it is no longer necessary to import natives at high cost or to send children to immersion courses in native territory. Thus, Korean families already send their children to English courses in China (Stevens & al. 2006), and Chinese institutions use Belgian teachers for English courses in their management schools (Graddol 2005). Secondly and even more importantly, as the number of (non-native) potential English speech partners expands along with the likelihood to meet them, there are more and more opportunities to speak, listen, read and write in English, and there is nothing like the expansion of costless opportunities to speak a language to cheapen the learning of it. Consequently, the swelling of the global cost of lingua franca learning is bound to be far less than proportional to the swelling of its amount.[4] At the limit, if it ever became as easy and natural to learn the lingua franca as it is to learn one's mother tongue, linguistic injustice, understood as the unfair distribution of the burdens of lingua franca production, would vanish altogether.

For the time being, however, the acquisition of the lingua franca at the present or at higher levels of proficiency does cost a considerable amount that needs to be shared. A country like the UK can fairly be expected to pay annually an amount that can be roughly assessed, in the light of the calculations sketched above, at €500 per capita and will increase or decrease over time depending on how fast the volume of learning increases and its unit cost decreases. A country like France, on the other hand, can fairly expect to receive annually a subsidy in the order of €25 per capita, which is likely to stagnate or fall over time, despite increased learning. This is more to pay for the UK and less to receive for France than if there had just been the two of them sharing half of the French learning costs (see Section 2), even tough both are much better off than in the latter situation because of lingua-franca-mediated worldwide communication. How do I propose implementing the transfer scheme thus shown to follow from linguistic justice, plausibly interpreted as proportionality between benefit and cost?

5.   A linguistic tax ?

Most straightforward would be to charge a global tax to the native English community and leave it to allocate this tax among its members, while distributing the proceeds among other linguistic communities so as to equalize all ratios of benefit to cost. But linguistic communities are not political communities, capable of taxing and of being taxed. Nor do they have the sort of grip on their members which religious communities may have. A more plausible though undeniably rougher approximation therefore consists in taxing countries, i.e. politically organized communities, in proportion to the number of English natives they house. One may, and probably should, exempt the countries with a small proportion of English natives, not only because this would not be worth the administrative trouble, but also because whatever English natives they have may be presumed to be particularly mobile, and hence likely to largely elude whatever allocation of the tax burden might be designed.

This leaves with a sizeable tax to be levied on the few countries in which the bulk of the English natives live — in particular the United States, home to 70% of them — and to be spread by these countries among their citizens. When distributing this tax, these countries may understandably balk at the prospect of targeting the native English speakers among their residents, if only because this would amount to perversely penalizing those families that assimilate most successfully. But in all cases where there is a significant degree of interaction between native English speakers and others, there would be little harm done in failing to differentiate between them for three reasons: first, whatever advantage the natives enjoy worldwide because of the lingua franca status will tend to spread to some extent to other people in their living environment; secondly, a public school system largely paid by natives is likely to provide language teaching to non-natives; and thirdly, the non-natives among natives enjoy particularly favourable conditions for learning the lingua franca, and hence should be entitled to a smaller transfer.

So far so good enough. But is it not pretty pointless to speculate about the way in which it would be most sensible to share out a tax that is most unlikely to ever come about. This is not the sort of tax that is going to be imposed by force. Hence, the governments of the Anglo countries will need to be persuaded — in English, of course — that this is a fair tax for them to pay. But how could they possibly be persuaded to provide massive subsidies for the learning of English all over the world, when such learning is happening anyway on a grand scale, powerfully driven by the individual and collective self-interest of hundreds of millions of people? A hopeless task, however you approach it, even if the governments concerned were able to understand and willing to accept that massive free riding on other people's efforts is ethically problematic. But perhaps we should not give up too quickly.

One possibility would be to bring the matter up whenever supranational organizations need to be financed. The most massive supranational budget is that of the European Union. For over twenty years the debate on the way in which contributions should be distributed between member states was dominated by the so-called "UK rebate" which Margaret Thatcher managed to bring home, after much bickering, in 1984. When part of it was cancelled and a new compromise was reached on this issue in December 2005, would it not have been appropriate to bring up the implicit transfer to the UK from the rest of the EU as a result of asymmetric language learning. The British rebate under discussion was in the order of 4.5 billion euros annually (see http://en.wikipedia.org/wiki/UK_rebate). But the 25 euros or so per capita to which the over 400 million EU citizens outside of the UK are entitled from the Anglo countries (see Section 4 above) amount to over 10 billion euros, while the 500 euros or so per capita owed by the 60 million UK citizens to non-Anglo communities around the world (see Section 4) amount to about 30 billion euros. So why not forget about the "UK rebate" and even ask a little additional effort. A fair contribution to the worldwide production of a mutually beneficial lingua franca requires far more to be done, by the Brits and others, in favour of non-Anglo communities throughout the world. But contributing an additional 10 billion euros to the EU budget would be a good start, while leaving the US, Canada, Australia, etc. to do equally good work in other continents.

6. Compensatory poaching

If this looks too haphazard, too dependent on contingent opportunities, what about compensatory free-riding? To understand the potential of this alternative avenue, first note that, as English increasingly suffices to get by wherever one is, both the incentive and opportunity to learn English will increase, whereas the incentive and opportunity to learn any other language will decrease. As a consequence, English will become more and more a globally public language. Other languages, by contrast, will remain or increasingly become globally private languages, not in the sense of being restricted to people's homes, but in the sense of being accessible to only a relatively small proportion of the people one has some chance of interacting with. Having no private language means being far more liable to give away information to any outsider who cares to listen or read. This may take some minor forms: whatever your mother tongue, you may benefit from overhearing two American tourists telling each other, in the queue to the museum, that the door to the toilet is locked. Had they been Finnish, you might have lost in vain your place in the queue.

Trivial asymmetric benefiting of this sort may seem hardly worth mentioning. But as more and more information gets loaded onto the web, easy to access, copy and use worldwide, this asymmetry is taking gigantic proportions. Whatever is being made available in this way to the three hundred million English natives is being made available simultaneously to the hundreds of millions of non-natives who bothered to learn English or are learning it now, and are massively over-represented among web users from their respective countries. By comparison, very little of the information that these hundreds of millions are putting on the web in their own native languages can be "overheard" by English natives (or indeed by the natives of any language but their own), because so few of these know other languages. Of course, more and more of the material put on the web by non-English natives will be in English (far from exclusively, or even mainly, to communicate with English natives). But as long as a significant proportion of potentially useful contents is produced and made available in other languages (see Nunberg 2002: 322–24), a deep asymmetry remains, which should partly cancel the advantage derived from one's language having become the lingua franca. Indeed, it may provide the only realistic chance of ever cancelling that advantage to a significant extent.

Whereas the political prospects of a trans-national linguistic tax are dim, it is trivial to observe that poaching — i.e. in this context accessing useful information without compensatory payment — is already happening on the web quite massively. The far greater difficulty of protecting intellectual property rights effectively on the web, compared to hard supports, means that such poaching, tolerated or not, will take ever growing proportions. In actual practice, by far the most effective (though selective) lock on information is the language in which it is expressed — for those who do not understand it. But as English spreads, all English material gets unlocked for the world, and poaching becomes increasingly asymmetric. True, when competence in English will have spread at a high level throughout the world, contents of more than local interest may be produced proportionally as much by non-English natives as by English natives, and the beneficiaries of the poaching will coincide with its victims. But this is fine if the trend suggested above (Section 4) materializes: by then, the learning of English will have cheapened to such an extent that there will be little to compensate for.

Of course, this is again only rough justice. For a start, even assuming all of the information accessed in this way is identified, it is not exactly easy to assess its value. And unless we do so, we are unable to state at some stage that the poaching of Anglo material by, say, the French must stop, because they have had access to their annual 1.5 billion euros quota (= €25 × 60 Mn) of free Anglo-produced material, in exchange for the language learning they do at their own expense for everyone's benefit. So, how should the material accessed be valued? The price the owners of the information are trying to get for it cannot serve as a standard of valuation: what is deliberately made accessible on the web free of charge should also enter the relevant accounts. How convenient or awkward it would be to make beneficiaries pay for a public good, or how keen or reluctant the producers of the public good are to avail themselves of this possibility, should in no way affect the assessment of the benefit level relevant to the application of our criterion of proportionality of benefit to cost. Nor is the fact that the information producers would have produced it even in the absence of an expectation of non-Anglo reward sufficient to make it count as nothing — just as the voluntary nature of language learning does not disqualify the possibility of free riding. Just as in the case of language learning something like the cost of production must be used. But the identification of the relevant part of the product is very problematic: in most cases, the product is indivisible and most of its beneficiaries are natives of the language in which it is expressed. The assessment of the size of the compensatory benefit, therefore, is unavoidably tricky.

Moreover might not the matching between the beneficiaries of the linguistic free riding and the victims of the compensatory free riding be very poor? Does it not amount to stealing blindly from a large number of people on the ground that some of them do not pay their due? Those who lose out through the plundering of the information they worked hard to produce may only very approximately coincide with those who benefit from the hard work that is being put worldwide into learning English. This lack of coincidence should not be exaggerated, and the poaching may be no less well targeted than the least badly targeted of all feasible schemes for taxing English natives. For the English native "symbol analysts" who are losing out in fees and royalties also tend to be among the cosmopolitans who most benefit in a wide variety of ways from the spreading of the lingua franca. And if less revenue can be collected abroad as a result of permissive legislation or lax enforcement in matters of intellectual property, they will have to recoup their costs and secure the profitability of their activities on Anglo territory, which will be a way of sharing the cost with a far wider constituency of English natives.

So, what is the bottom line? That this is the least bad way of organizing fair compensation, even though it will be necessarily be messy. Free access to English-language contents on the web — or indeed in (increasingly obsolete) printed form — can plausibly be advocated on grounds of justice. When no intellectual property rights protect them, no moral self-restraint should be exercised. When intellectual property rights do protect them, no vigorous efforts should be deployed to enforce them in non-Anglo countries. Nor can collaboration be legitimately expected for the sake of redressing the resulting asymmetric (net) benefiting by non-English natives and non-Anglo countries. For this is nothing but compensatory (if not retaliatory) free riding, a rough compensation for the massive benefit offered free of charge to the natives of the lingua franca by the hard learning of non-natives. To put it metaphorically: when it is in everyone's interest that one should always meet in the same place, it is fair that those who never need to do any travelling should be charged part of the travelling expenses. If they cannot feasibly or conveniently be charged, they can fairly be expected to compensate by offering dinner. And if they do not bother, the others are entitled to help themselves on their shelves.

As the very spreading of the lingua franca makes its learning less hard, less compensatory poaching will be justified in this spirit. But less asymmetric poaching will be happening anyway, because of more and more English content coming from non-English natives. It does not follow that the poaching must then stop. We might as well enjoy the lingua franca to the full, while resisting or circumventing any attempt by greedy fingers to lock what is no longer linguistically locked, to fetter the free worldwide flow of knowledge and ideas to which the spread of a global lingua franca will be giving a wonderful unprecedented boost.

Notes

1. The present paper draws on the final part of Chapter 2 of a book in progress under the title *Linguistic Justice for Europe and for the World* (Oxford University Press.). Other parts of that chapter provide an argument for the chosen principle, and other chapters of the book deal with linguistic injustice in the two senses ignored here. A preliminary exploration of linguistic justice as cooperative justice can be found in Van Parijs (2002) and de Briey & Van Parijs (2002) and a more general discussion of linguistic justice in all three senses in Van Parijs (2004).

2. This criterion happens to be a specific version of the "rule of distributive justice" formulated by George Homans (1961: 72–8, 232–64) and subsequently used in the social-psychological

literature under the name of "equity". Homans's conjecture is that in many contexts of human cooperation (or "exchange") feelings of fairness and resentment are guided by a rule of proportionality between investment and profit, with investment understood very broadly to cover age, seniority or gender as well as effort or skills. Many interpretations of "investment" allowed by Homans (such as age or gender) are too morally arbitrary to make ethical sense. Moreover, even when they are filtered out (leaving us with something like "effort"), Homan's rule does not provide us with an acceptable criterion of *distributive* justice (see Van Parijs 1995: 166–9 and 281 fn87). But this need not prevent it from providing a plausible criterion of cooperative justice, with a fair distribution of entitlements taken as a given background.

3. A thorough study by Grin (2005: 88–91) concludes that the annual per capita cost of foreign language teaching in state schools is about €36 in 2002–3 in the UK, compared to about €138 in 2003–4 in France (about 10% of the total annual education budget). In the United States, over half of secondary school pupils no longer study any foreign language and the cost of foreign language learning per capita can be roughly estimated to be about forty times less than in Switzerland (Maurais 2003: 24, 32).

4. This process can be expected to be far slower in bigger linguistic communities, which provide less opportunity (and hence also motivation) for interacting in the lingua franca. More than linguistic distance, this is a reason why the learning cost of the Chinese is likely to remain particularly high, and hence justify a higher share of the subsidies than what is justified by the sheer arithmetic effect of the size of the Chinese linguistic community.

References

de Briey, L. & Van Parijs, P. 2002. La justice linguistique comme justice coopérative, *Revue de philosophie économique* 5: 5–37.

Graddol, D. 2005. Language trends and scenarios: Views from Western Europe, intervention at the conference Language Policy Aspects of the Expansion of the European Union, Vilnius (Lithuania) 30:7–1/8/2006.

Grin, F. 2005. *L'Enseignement des langues étrangères comme politique publique*. Paris: Haut Conseil de l'Evaluation de l'Ecole, Rapport n°19, septembre 2005, 131p. http://www.ladocumentationfrancaise.fr/rapports-publics/054000678/index.shtml

Homans, G.C. 1961 [1973]. *Social Behaviour. Its elementary forms*. London: Routledge & Kegan Paul.

Maurais, J. 2003. Towards a new global linguistic order?. In *Languages in a Globalising World*, J. Maurais & M.A. Morris (eds), 13–36. Cambridge: CUP.

Nunberg, G. 2002. Langues et communautés linguistiques à l'époque du discours électronique. In *La Politique de Babel. Du monolinguisme d'état au plurilinguisme des peuples*, D. Lacorne & T. Judt (eds), 321–343. Paris: Karthala.

Piron, C. 2001. L'Européen trilingue: Un espoir réaliste ? In *L'Europe parlera-t-elle anglais demain?*, R. Chaudenson (ed.), 93–102. Paris: Institut de la francophonie & L'Harmattan.

Stevens, G., Jin, K. & Song H.J. 2006. Short-term migration and the acquisition of a world language. *International Migration* 44(1): 167–79.

Van Parijs, P. 1995a. *Real Freedom for All. What (if anything) is wrong with capitalism?* Oxford: OUP.

Van Parijs, P. 2002. Linguistic Justice. *Politics, Philosophy and Economics* 1 (1): 59–74. (Also in *Language Rights and Political Theory*, W. Kymlicka & A. Patten (eds), 153–68, OUP, 2003).
Van Parijs, P. 2004. Europe's Linguistic Challenge. *Archives européennes de sociologie* 45(1): 111–52.

Author's address

Chaire Hoover d'éthique économique et sociale
3 Place Montesquieu
1348 Louvain-la-Neuve
Belgium

philippe.vanparijs@uclouvain.be

Appendices

1. An estimate of the Anglo fair share in today's learning cost

300 million English natives and one hundred communities of 60 million non-English natives each, 10% of which have learned English: this gives us a very simple first approximation of the sort of world we are in or shall be in shortly. What sort of share of the total cost of learning should we expect Anglophones to bear under these assumptions? It is given by the ratio of the benefit for the 300 million Anglophones of acquiring 600 million additional speech partners to the benefit for 600 million non-Anglophones of each acquiring as speech partners 300 million Anglophones and 594 million non-Anglophones (the other learners minus those with whom they shared their mother tongue), i.e.

$$(300 \times 600)/((300 \times 600) + 100 \times (6 \times (300 + (600 - 6)))) = 25.1\%.$$

Assuming, in line with François Grin's (2005) estimate used in the text, that the cost of turning 10% of one's population into competent English speakers amounts to about €100 per capita per annum, this means a subsidy of €25.1 per capita for each learning country, and a tax of €25.1 × (6000/300) = €502.0 per capita for the Anglo population.

As the lingua franca gradually spreads further to cover the whole of mankind, the total cost (with an unchanged unit cost) will be multiplied by ten (from 600 to 6000 million learners), while the Anglophones' fair share in this cost will be divided by five (from 25.1% to 4.58%).

However, the non-Anglo linguistic communities are not of equal sizes. This matters to some extent for the size of the total subsidy and matters a great deal more for its distribution. To see this, consider a somewhat more realistic distribution between linguistic communities, say 300 Mn native English speakers, and 10% of secondary English speakers in one linguistic community of 1000 Mn (say, the Chinese), in 50 linguistic communities of 60 Mn speakers (say, the French, etc.) and 500 linguistic communities of 4Mn speakers (say, the Danes, etc.).

The total benefit is then given by

$$(300 \times 600) + 1 \times (100 \times (300 + 500)) + 50 \times (6 \times (300 + 100 + 494)) + 500 \times (0.4 \times (300 + 100 + 499.6)) = 180000 + 80000 + 268200 + 179920 = 708120.$$ With a per capita cost of 100 (relative to the total population), the overall ratio of benefit to cost is then $708120/(6000 \times 100) = 1.18$.

The pre-transfer ratios of benefit to cost (with the assumed 10% ratio of learners to total population) are

$0.1 \times (300 + 500))/100 = 0.800$ for the Chinese
$0.1 \times (300 + 100 + 494)/100 = 0.894$ for the French
$0.1 \times (300 + 100 + 499.6)/100 = 0.8996$ for the Danes.

As all three ratios fall short of the overall ratio of benefit to cost, all learning linguistic communities will be entitled to part of the subsidy to be paid by the Anglo community. Adding another lot of communities of no more than even, say, a single English-learning member would hardly alter the picture: even they (who stand to gain most from widespread lingua franca learning) would have a benefit cost ratio that does not exceed 0.9. However, the level of the subsidy varies as a decreasing function of how many partners the lingua franca enables a linguistic community to gain. Thus, the per capita subsidies are

€32.20 $(= -(80 - 100 \times 1.18)/1.18)$ for the Chinese,
€24.24 $(= -(89.4 - 100 \times 1.18)/1.18)$ for the French,
€23.76 $(= -(89.96 - 100 \times 1.18)/1.18)$ for the Danes,

instead of a uniform subsidy of €25.1 under the assumption of 100 linguistic communities of equal sizes. With 16.7% of the learners, the Chinese can claim 21.1% $(= 1000 \times 32.20/300 \times 508.13)$ of the total subsidy, even taking no account of the linguistic distance between Chinese and English.

The Anglo population's per capita liability, on the other hand, needs to rise to €508.13 $(= (1000 \times 32.20 + 3000 \times 24.24 + 2000 \times 23.76)/300)$ i.e. slighly more than under the assumption of equal sizes (€502) in order to yield the same ratio of benefit to cost for English natives as for everyone else: $600/508.13 = 1.18$.

2. When the lingua franca becomes universal

Applied to the real world, the ratios assumed in our illustration would reflect a very minimalist estimate of the spreading of English (with the population of English learners double the population of English natives). If instead we consider the extreme situation in which the whole population of the world has learned English as a second language, the proportion of the cost that could fairly be billed to the Anglophones would — paradoxically perhaps — shrink dramatically.

With rough estimates of the populations of English natives (say 300 Mn) and non-English natives (say, 6000 Mn) in today's world, the Anglo countries' minimum fair share in the cost of lingua franca learning is given by the ratio of the benefit to Anglophones of universal English learning (300Mn × 6000 Mn) to the total benefit (300Mn × 6000 Mn + 6300Mn × 6000Mn), i.e. $300/(6600) = 1/22 = 4.5\%$. This corresponds to the extreme case where there are 6 billion different languages (and hence learning the lingua franca enables each non-English native to communicate with 6 billion minus 1 other non-English natives).

But it cannot be expected to be much higher in the real world. With a more realistic approximation of 100 non-Anglo communities of 60 million people each, the cost-sharing required from the Anglophones becomes $(300 \times 6000)/((300 \times 6000) + 100(60 \times (300 + (6000 - 60)))) = 4.58\%$.

With 10 communities of 600 million people each, it rises to exactly $(300 \times 6000)/((300 \times 6000) + 10(600 \times (300 + (6000 - 600)))) = 5.0\%$.

The reason is simply that, even in this last case, the bulk of the benefit to each non-Anglo community comes from being able to communicate, thanks to English, with other non-Anglo communities.

Hence, as the lingua franca becomes more and more universal, the proportion of its cost to be borne by its natives decreases very steeply. Under realistic assumptions about the degree of diversity in the non Anglo population, it will eventually fall below 5%.

However, it does not follow that the absolute level of the cost to be borne by the Anglo community, whether in the aggregate or per capita, will fall as an ever greater proportion of the world population learns the lingua franca. For as the Anglophone community's share of the cost shrinks with every increase in the number of learners, the total learning cost increases even more with every such increase, and the Anglophone community's aggregate contribution to the cost and its per capita contribution are therefore bound to increase in absolute terms, though at a decreasing rate as the total number of lingua franca learners becomes large relative to the number of lingua franca natives. Or at least this conclusion follows if the unit cost of learning is not affected by the very spread of English, an assumption questioned in Section 4.

3. Where are we heading?

To see which way we are moving, it is useful to consider the limiting case where 100% of the world population learns English (as in Appendix 2), while heeding the fact that the world's linguistic communities vary greatly in sizes (as at the end of Appendix 1).

The overall ratio of benefit to cost is then given by

$$(300 \times 6000) + 1 \times (1000 \times (300 + 5000)) + 50 \times (60 \times (300 + 1000 + 4940)) + 500 \times (4 \times (300 + 1000 + 4996))/(6000 \times 1000) = 6.40.$$

The per capita subsidies now diverge far more widely than with a smaller percentage of learners (see Appendix 1) because, except for the Chinese, the learning of the lingua franca now gives access to over 99% of the world population:

€172.13 (= −(5300 − 1000 × 6.402)/6.402) for the Chinese,
€ 25.30 (= −(6240 − 1000 × 6.402)/6.402) for the French,
€ 16.58 (= −(6296 − 1000 × 6.402)/6.402) for the Danes,

instead of a uniform subsidy of €1000 × 4.58 = €45.8 under our equal size assumption (see Appendix 2). With 16.7% of the learners, the Chinese alone now absorb 61.2% (= 1000 × 172.13/300 × 937.3) of the fair subsidy, even abstracting from the fact that they may have greater difficulty learning English than many others.

The Anglo population's per capita liability correspondingly rises to €937.30 (= (1000 × 172.13 + 3000 × 25.30 + 2000 × 16.58)/300) i.e. again somewhat more than under the assumption of equal sizes (€45.8 × 6000/300 = €916.0), and considerably more than if only 10% are learning. Yet, because of the massively enhanced benefit resulting from the universalisation of the lingua franca, this is consistent with English natives getting the same ratio of benefit to cost as everyone else: 600/937.30 = 6.40.

Assessing efficiency and fairness in multilingual communication

Towards a general analytical framework

Michele Gazzola and François Grin
Université de Genève, Switzerland

The comparison between various language policies that aim to manage multilingual communication ought to rely on some robust methodology for evaluation. This paper discusses the possibility to found such a methodology on the well-established concepts of efficiency and fairness. Assessing efficiency implies comparing how resources are allocated under alternative policy options (or scenarios) in order to identify the policy promising the best overall allocation. Assessing fairness calls for the evaluation of the distributive effects of each scenario on the linguistic groups involved in communication — that is, ascertaining who benefits and who loses (and how much) under alternative policy options.

This paper provides the background for developing indicators of effective and fair communication, which synthesise some desirable characteristics of communication processes. They enable us to compare different ways of handling communication in multilingual settings. In order to assess effectiveness and efficiency, we work with three (not mutually exclusive) definitions of communication, namely, informatory, cooperative and strategic communication. These definitions reflect the different (main) communicational intents of the actors. In order to assess fairness, we establish a distinction between communication in terms of access, process and outcome.

Introduction

In the case of scientific communication, to which this issue of the *AILA Review* is devoted, linguistic equality can be studied from different perspectives. The approach we present in this article banks on the economics of language and language policy evaluation, a field of research with a strong interdisciplinary orientation (see e.g. Grin, 1996, 2003). The theoretical background and the methodologies for evaluation are imported from policy analysis (Rossi *et al.*, 2004, and Dunn, 2004), and welfare economics (Boadway and Bruce, 1984, and Just *et al.*, 2004), a branch of economic theory

AILA Review 20 (2007), 87–105. DOI 10.1075/aila.20.08gaz
ISSN 1461–0213 / E-ISSN 1570–5595 © John Benjamins Publishing Company

that is concerned with the evaluation of economic policies in terms of their effects and implications on the well-being of society. The main advantage of developing an analytical framework based on these disciplines is that it provides a robust methodology for *evaluation*, and more specifically, for the comparison between alternative scenarios. The very fact of looking for alternatives implies that some scenarios can be considered preferable to others, and that we therefore need explicit criteria and a consistent methodology to rank-order the alternatives considered. Two main criteria in economic and policy analysis are particularly relevant for the comparison between alternative scenarios, namely, efficiency and fairness.

The purpose of this paper is to present some guidelines towards a general analytical framework for assessing the relative efficiency and fairness of different ways of managing multilingual communication, or more specifically, communication occurring in multilingual organisations (including not only international organisations, but also academic institutions, multilingual companies, etc.) dealing with linguistic diversity both for their internal and external communication. This focus on multilingual organisations does not imply any major loss of generality, since the principles and the methodology of the policy analysis approach have a broad practical applicability that extends, *mutatis mutandis*, to other areas of linguistic diversity management.

In this paper, we proceed as follows: Section 1 presents the concepts of efficiency and fairness, as they are employed in economics and policy analysis. This section serves as an epistemological introduction to Sections 2 and 3. These sections outline some principles of efficiency (Section 2) and fairness (Section 3) evaluation in multilingual communication. Section 4 sums up our main results in a brief conclusion.

Allocation, distribution and evaluation

The problem of how social resources should be used arises when they are scarce and have alternative uses. In economics, the term "resource" usually refers to financial (or material) resources, but non-material, symbolic values are equally conceptually relevant to an economic analysis and ought, in principle, to be taken into account as well. Efficiency, therefore, refers to resource allocation, and in particular to how resources should be employed to get as much output as possible out of a certain amount of resources used (see Myles, 1995 for a more technical definition). As such, the concept of efficiency can be applied to a broad range of human activities. Without entering into technical detail, we shall simply recall that, in general, resources are allocated more efficiently in state B than in state A if in B no one in society is worse off — that is, no one's "utility" (or well-being) decreases — and at least one individual is better off than in state A. In other words, there is room for a more efficient use of resources if a re-allocation of resources makes at least one person better off without making anyone worse off; this rule is known as the "Pareto criterion".

Clearly, this general principle is of limited applicability, since the situations in which a change does not harm any member of society are relatively unusual. Compensatory transfers are a possible solution, in the sense that those who benefit from the change pay a compensation to those who lose, so that in the aggregate no one is worse off. These transfers might not be easy to implement in practice (cf. Boardman *et al.*, 2006: Just *et al.*, 2004). There is, however, a less demanding version of this principle that has broader practical applicability. According to this criterion — called the Kaldor-Hicks criterion — an improvement in resource allocation is possible if those who are better off in state *B can* (but not necessarily do) fully compensate those who are made worse off, and ultimately at least one person is better off.

The notion of efficiency is particularly important in the evaluation of state intervention, which typically takes the form of public policy. Decision-makers are interested in the evaluation of the impacts of a given policy on the well-being of the members of society. The Kaldor-Hicks criterion provides guidelines to assess whether a project (such as, for example, the construction of a new underground line) can be justified on the basis of efficiency.

However, the Kaldor-Hicks criterion does not require that those who benefit from a particular policy *actually* compensate those who lose. It simply requires that compensation is *potentially* possible and that, in the aggregate (that is, if compensatory transfers were eventually made), no one would be worse off. Nevertheless, as the choice about whether or not compensation is finally paid is a political question, "an appropriate welfare analysis must investigate the effects of a policy change on both groups and leave the subjective evaluation of which distribution is better to the policy maker who is elected to fulfil that responsibility" (Just *et al.*, 2004: 8).

The issue of fairness becomes relevant at this stage.[1] One of the most important tasks of the analyst in the evaluation process, whether carried out *ex-ante* or *ex-post*, is to point out the distributive consequences of alternative scenarios. In other words, almost every change is likely to affect asymmetrically the relative position of the relevant groups — whether the latter are defined on a socio-economic or ethno-linguistic basis — so that some groups win and some groups lose, or at least, they do not win to the same extent. It is part of the work of the analyst to characterise these groups, to identify the winners and the losers (or alternatively the big and the small winners) and to identify the magnitude of gains and losses caused by a particular change.

As a result, even if a particular policy could be justified on the basis of the Kaldor-Hicks criterion (efficiency), it is perfectly possible for it to be eventually rejected for reasons of equity. In other words, as fairness is a key element of policy evaluation too, there is no reason why a policy intervention fulfilling the Kaldor-Hicks criterion should not be rejected because of its unfair distributive consequences — it may, for example, be rejected on the grounds that no compensation between groups is technically feasible.

In this paper, therefore, we do not refer to "fairness" in moral terms, that is, in terms of compliance of a give policy to certain ethical principles, but rather in terms of the distributive consequences that alternative policies entail (cf. Zajac, 1995, Mueller, 2003, and Moulin, 2003). The choice of whether inequalities should be accepted or not is a political matter. As such, it cannot be made on purely technical grounds and must be the object of a democratic public debate that typically relies, explicitly or not, on alternative theories of justice (cf. Arnsperger and van Parijs, 2000, and Kymlicka, 2002). However, the evaluation work carried out by the policy analyst can contribute to this debate by making it a better informed one.

Efficient communication as an object of study

The limits of cost-benefits analysis for language policy evaluation

Language-related policies, such as the promotion of a minority language or the teaching of foreign languages, can also be assessed in terms of their efficiency and fairness (Grin, 2005). Note, however, that the principle of comparison between alternatives and the techniques for evaluation of efficiency and fairness can be adapted to a broader range of situations in human life. For this reason the term "alternative policies" is used here to stress this principle of comparison between competing scenarios, whether they are taken at a state level or at the level of a more simple organisation.

One of the most popular techniques to assess the relative efficiency of different policy alternatives is cost-benefit analysis or CBA (cf. Brent, 1997, and Boardman *et al.*, 2006). CBA is based on a systematic comparison of the levels of *net* benefit of alternative projects (this term is generally used in CBA literature as equivalent to "policy" or "programme"), the net benefit being defined as the difference between gross benefits and costs. In principle, the existence of a positive net benefit is the necessary condition for compensating those who are worse off because of a given policy (see above). If several projects have a positive net benefit, CBA suggests, all other things being equal, picking the project offering the largest net benefit.

In order to have a reliable basis for comparison, the net benefits of alternative programmes must be expressed in a common unit of measurement, usually money. In principle, "symbolic" values can also be taken into account to a certain extent, provided that the people concerned accept to state truthfully how much they are willing to pay for those things to which they attach symbolic value (cf. Grin and Vaillancourt, 1997). A standard textbook example is that of environmental assets, such as a beautiful panorama that one can enjoy from the terrace of one's home. If watching the sunset is valuable to a particular person, she will be willing to pay a higher price for a flat with a view than for a ground floor one overlooking the parking lot. The difference in this person's willingness-to-pay for these two otherwise identical flats can be considered a good approximation of the value that she attaches to a beautiful view from her terrace.

In principle, a similar logic could be applied to the comparison between alternative language policies, such as the promotion of the language of immigrants in the school system of a given territory, *by comparison with* a strictly monolingual system. The usefulness of a comparison between the costs and benefits of alternative language policies has already been stressed by Jernudd (1971) and more recently, among others, by Grin (1994), Vaillancourt (1995) for bilingualism in Canada, Patrinos and Velez (1995) for bilingual education in Guatemala, Mühlhäusler and Damania (2004) for indigenous languages in Australia, and by several contributions in Ricento (2006). Take for example the hypothetical case of the introduction of an immigrant language in the school system of a given country. This policy entails both costs like the training of teachers, and benefits, some of them strictly material, such as those accruing to those who will in the future use this language for business with countries where it is spoken, while others are symbolic benefits, such as maintaining cultural links with the language of their relatives.

To sum up, the analyst should: (i) identify relevant benefits and costs; (ii) quantify in monetary units all the benefits and costs previously identified and compute the net benefit of each option; (iii) compare the two (or more) alternative options and choose that with the larger net benefit. The logical rigour of CBA, therefore, comes at a price. First, the identification of the possible channels through which languages are potentially carriers of benefits or costs is far from clear. Some relationships — like that between language skills and wage differentials on the labour market — have been modelled formally (cf. Grin, 2005: 35–45 for a review), but there is still much to do at a theoretical level. Moreover, moving from the formal model to the empirical estimation requires a considerable amount of data, and most of them are usually not collected or simply not available.

These conceptual and empirical difficulties are even greater when dealing with large-scale phenomena, such as language policies to promote multilingualism in Europe or to "internationalise" post-graduate education. This does not, however, mean that the entire endeavour of evaluation is hopeless, but simply that some simplifications are necessary, a question to which we now turn.

Assessing effectiveness

For the purposes of analysing multilingual communication in multilingual organisations, we shall focus on one particular, but significant, benefit that is always mentioned in the literature, namely, communication, and, in particular, *effective* communication. In essence, this approach is an adaptation of the principle of comparison between alternative scenarios to the field of communication. By adopting this approach, we are implicitly making the following assumptions. One is, that the degree of efficiency and the distributive effects of different models of management of multilingual communication, according to their more or less high level of diversity, (i) *are* intrinsically relevant questions; (ii) are related to more or less high degrees of efficiency and to the distributive effects in the broader linguistic environment[2] (of which communication is clearly a key element). Putting it differently, we are assuming that the part is a barometer for the whole.

Let us now turn to the question of what effective (multilingual) communication means. Let us stress that we are focusing on communication mediated through language (or rather, language*s*), since our main concern is not communication *per se*, but communication occurring in multilingual settings. Hence, other communicational means such as symbols or gestural expressiveness will not be considered here. Should we focus on the most skeletal definition of communication, that is, the mere transmission of information? Or should we work with a "thicker" definition? A possible strategy is not to choose between them, and to use jointly several definitions that are not necessarily mutually exclusive. These reflect different perspectives on the nature and functions of communication. More specifically, we assume that three different definitions of communication should be taken into account. These definitions have been inspired in particular by the contributions of Paulré (1993) and enriched with the work of Carey (1992), Charaudeau (1995) and Lamizet and Silem (1997). Let us call them:

α.   *informatory communication*
β.   *cooperative communication*
γ.   *strategic communication*

It is worth stressing that we are not proposing an abridged or revised version of the well-known Jakobsonian communication functions. Rather, by using these definitions we aim at stressing the (main) *intent* of a communication occurring between people (or groups of people) speaking different languages. Clearly, distinct communicational intents will be related to the utilisation of some particular functions. However, the identification and the description of these functions in multilingual contexts are not central to our discussion and will not be examined here.

It is important to understand that we are *not* talking about actual communication in its full complexity, and that we are *not* assuming that communication can ever be reduced to any of these types. Simply, we propose to look at selected aspects of communication, in order to allow for comparison between different occurrences of communication in professional activity.

The concept of "main communicational intent" must be interpreted in the light therefore of a given *context* (that is, a communicational situation or perhaps more generally an "interactional situation"). The point of departure for the analyst's observations is the core activities carried out in a given organisation or in a particular part of it. What characterises a communication as effective, therefore, is its direct relationship with the attainment of the main *goals* of the activities observed (e.g. to cooperate in the case of a work meeting, or to convince in the case of a Member of the European Parliament making a speech, etc.).

Let us now take a closer look at the three definitions. In the first definition (α), communication is regarded as a process of transmission of contents between actors (in our case, between individuals belonging to different language groups). Communication, therefore, amounts to an exchange of information similar to that occurring between computers. This definition is certainly the most reductionist of the three, but nevertheless it seems to have gained large currency in the public debate. For example, it is the definition implicitly referred to by most of the commentators who see languages as mere (and perfectly substitutable) tools (e.g. de Swaan 2001).

The key point in this case is to assess when "informatory" communication among people of different languages is "effective". To answer to this question, a possible strategy is to devise a set of *indicators* that serve to characterise an instance of communication as effective. In other words, indicators should be designed in such a way to *reflect* some "desirable characteristics" that communication should have to be effective, that is, to effectively transmit information in a given context.

Let us take the example of a simple indicator in the case of an international meeting of people belonging to different language groups. An α-communication between individuals is effective if the transmission of information occurs without substantial losses or "noise". Assuming that interpretation and translation services are used, a possible indicator of effectiveness is the inverse of the number of errors due to errors in interpretation. One point needs to be clarified with respect to the use of indicators of effectiveness. Their main function is not to assess whether a specific way of handling multilingual communication is efficient *per se*, but to *compare* different alternatives. In other words, what is relevant for the comparative analysis is to understand how an indicator such as the inverse of the number of errors *changes* when we move from, say, a full symmetrical system of interpretation and translation to, say, a system that uses the relay technique.[3] Of course, the use of indicators is not risk-free. We shall come back to this point in the conclusion.

In the second definition (β), communication is seen as an activity through which cooperation and coordination become possible. This definition refers to the idea that communicating also means having something "in common", be it culture or a feeling of membership in a given organisation. Therefore, communication is effective if it encourages the attainment of some shared or common objectives of the groups involved. This definition of communication largely includes the first definition, and thus they do not have to be regarded as antithetical. Take the case of an international scientific meeting on the effects of smoking on health. If there is genuine participation and cooperation in the debate, and assuming away other differences between agents, we should not observe significant inequalities in an indicator such as the speaking time of the participants according to their language group (of course, this indicator must be adjusted for the size of groups).

The third definition of communication (strategic or γ), emphasizes the power (or "cratic") aspect of communication. Communication here is defined as an activity intended to persuade, influence or charm others. In this case, therefore, we stress the role of communication both as a tool and object of competition for power between actors or even organisations that aim to achieve their own goals. Take the example of an academic institution confronted with the challenge of internationalisation and student mobility. A γ-communication aimed at the external world, in this case towards students, is effective if it helps to reach the institution's own objectives, such as persuading as many students as possible to enrol. A possible effectiveness indicator of γ-communication can be the actual number of enrolments. Note again that the real question is not to assess the value of the indicator as such, but to see how it changes if the university moves from, say, a situation in which only a language is used for undergraduate teaching to another in which a mix of two languages is employed.

In this case too, α-communication is to a large extent included in the definition of strategic communication, since the transmission of information is part of the persuasive communicational activity. The cooperative and the strategic dimensions of communication are not necessarily mutually exclusive either. For example, both may be present in those activities that lead to a common agreement. However, it is useful to keep these definitions distinct, first because this difference is likely to play a role in the evaluation of fairness, and secondly, because the effectiveness indicators designed are not necessarily the same.

A useful methodological distinction in the evaluation is that between communication occurring within the organisation or institution (which we shall call "internal") and communication from the organisation towards the external environment ("external"). There is no reason why effectiveness indicators for internal and external communication should be the same.

Summing up, the effectiveness of alternative systems for managing multilingual communication can be assessed across two dimensions, namely, external and internal communication, and across three different main communicational intents, namely, informatory, cooperative and strategic. This yields a possible set of effectiveness indicators like that showed in Table 1.

Table 1. Matrix of effectiveness indicators

Internal communication (i)			External communication (e)		
Main Communicational intent	Indicators	Vector of indicators	Main Communicational intent	Indicators"	Vector of indicators
α	$\alpha^i_1, \alpha^i_2, ..., \alpha^i_a$	$[\alpha^i]$	α	$\alpha^e_1, \alpha^e_2, ..., \alpha^e_a$	$[\alpha^e]$
β	$\beta^i_1, \beta^i_2, ..., \beta^i_b$	$[\beta^i]$	β	$\beta^e_1, \beta^e_2, ..., \beta^e_b$	$[\beta^e]$
γ	$\gamma^i_1, \gamma^i_2, ..., \gamma^i_c$	$[\gamma^i]$	γ	$\gamma^e_1, \gamma^e_2, ..., \gamma^e_c$	$[\gamma^e]$

The number of indicators is not necessarily equal for every cell. This idea is captured by the subscripts (a, b, c) for different classes of indicators of type α, β, or γ, and by the superscript (e, i) which is used to distinguish indicators used for internal communication from those employed for internal communication.

The main function of this matrix is just to help the analyst to come up with an analytical frame for the management of multilingual communication, and therefore it should not be seen as an attempt to "measure" communication. Besides, this matrix is just a stepping stone towards the core activity of the policy analyst, namely *comparison* (see below).

The theoretical elaboration and refinement of these indicators is an intellectual challenge that has to be tackled in an interdisciplinary perspective, in which applied linguists and sociolinguists play a very central role. We shall come back to this point in our conclusions. The result of such an effort will ideally be a set of reliable and relevance indicators that, according to the context analysed, can be used in comparative analysis.

Comparing scenarios: effectiveness

In order to carry out a comparative analysis, the possible alternatives must be spelled out. Comparative analysis makes no sense if no appropriate *counterfactual* is specified, and the *status quo* is the simplest possible type of counterfactual.

The system for handling multilingual communication observed at time t_1 in a given context, therefore, should be characterised in terms of its level of linguistic diversity (say, D_1). This characterisation can be made by using several analytical dimensions (or parameters), such as the number of languages used. Clearly, the list can be enlarged and refined by adding new dimensions of linguistic diversity. For this purpose, House and Rehbein (2004: 3) provide a useful general list of parameters:[4]

-   the languages used (L1 to L_n);
-   the speech situations (differentiated according to discourse and text);[5]
-   the roles of the participants (with or without language mediators);
-   the socio-political status of the languages involved (languages in relation to whole society as a whole, including L1, second or foreign language(s), *lingua franca*, etc.);
-   the skills of the participants (from individuals to groups, in a continuum from monolingual to multilingual);
-   the typological distance between the languages involved;
-   the degree of language separation, language mixing or switching.

Not all conceivable systems of multilingual management are equally interesting; moreover, the number of possible combinations may be exceedingly high and make the analysis unmanageable. Thus, a reasonable strategy is to compare two alternatives to the *status quo*. The first alternative may be defined by a level of diversity (say, D_L) lower than D_1, and the second by a level of diversity (say, D_H) higher than D_1. As the object of study is multilingual communication, and more specifically, efficiency in multilingual communication management, the comparison should be framed in terms of different *levels* of linguistic diversity.

The alternatives D_L and D_H must include all the parameters used to characterise D_1 (for example, the simple number of languages). Note, however, that changing all the parameters at the same time is not necessary for characterising D_L and D_H with respect to D_1, since one may decide to focus only on the change of a subset of parameters. D_L and D_H may be real, but also ideal alternatives, specifically designed to highlight some specific features that are particularly relevant to the comparison. For example, we might compare a strictly monolingual firm to a company working with three languages.

D_L and D_H are levels of diversity that the organisations are potentially interested in targeting for their internal or external communication. However, assuming that organisations are able to target different levels of linguistic diversity is not the same as assuming that they are able to modify the surrounding linguistic environment at will. The behaviour of organisations, of course, can contribute to alter some of the characteristics of the linguistic environment — even if such a change is not the deliberate *aim* of the action taken. But this is not the main point here. What counts is that they are able to modify their language policy regarding external communication and to change some internal characteristics; this gives rise to what we shall also call competing "scenarios".

In the main, the comparative analysis consists in assessing how the value of effectiveness indicators shown in Table 1 is modified if the scenario changes from the *status quo* (D_1) to D_H, or alternatively, to D_L. In the example mentioned before, this is equivalent to asking how an indicator of type γ^e (say, γ^e_1, the number of students enrolled) changes if we move from a situation D_1 — in which undergraduate programmes are taught in one language only — to another situation D_H — in which two languages are employed. The expected output of the comparative work would be a set of indicators arranged as in Table 2.

Table 2. Comparative analysis matrix

Less diversity (D_L)		*Status quo* (D_1)		More diversity (D_H)	
Internal communication	External communication	Internal communication	External communication	Internal communication	External communication
$[\alpha^i]_L$	$[\alpha^e]_L$	$[\alpha^i]_1$	$[\alpha^e]_1$	$[\alpha^i]_H$	$[\alpha^e]_H$
$[\beta^i]_L$	$[\beta^e]_L$	$[\beta^i]_1$	$[\beta^e]_1$	$[\beta^i]_H$	$[\beta^e]_H$
$[\gamma^i]_L$	$[\gamma^e]_L$	$[\gamma^i]_1$	$[\gamma^e]_1$	$[\gamma^i]_H$	$[\gamma^e]_H$

Ideally, comparative analysis would require an experimental design method or multivariate analysis allowing us to isolate exogenous effects. However, these methods are unlikely to be applicable in practice because of the complex interconnections between the processes at hand and the difficulty of gathering highly detailed and mutually comparable data. Nevertheless, circumstantial analysis based on current or past data, interviews, as well as sociolinguistic research, all provide useful inputs making it possible to estimate orders of magnitude, with which much policy-making has to be content in practice. As a general rule, some information is better than no information at all — once the analytical procedures adopted are clearly spelled out — and in many real-world situations, it is reasonable to aim at plausibility rather than formal statistical significance.

Comparing scenarios: efficiency

Comparing alternative scenarios simply on the basis of the indicators of their respective effectiveness will be misleading, because every "effect" is achieved at a certain cost. The comparison between alternatives, therefore, should not be limited to the comparison between effectiveness indicators, but it should also include an assessment of the costs of each alternative. A useful evaluation technique is *cost-effectiveness analysis* (CEA). CEA is preferred to CBA in many domains, such as health care, in which for several reasons (ethical, practical, etc.) it is unsatisfactory to attach a monetary value to benefits. CEA compares alternative projects on the basis of their costs and effects. The effect is measured in some non-monetary form (say, time, the number of potential customers, etc.), while the cost is measured in monetary form. What is relevant for the comparative analysis is the ratio between the costs and the effect measured through a given indicator. This ratio is called cost-effectiveness ratio (CE ratio). Without entering into technical detail (cf. Levin and MacEwan, 2001), suffice it to say that to assess the *efficiency* of alternative projects, the analyst ranks-order them according to their cost-effectiveness (CE) ratios, which, for the purposes of this paper, amounts to treating "cost-effectiveness" and "efficiency" as synonyms.[6] The lower the CE ratio, the more efficient the policy. In other words, all other things being equal, the policy with the lowest CE ratio is that by which we can obtain a unit of effect (e.g., an additional potential customer) at the lowest cost per unit.

Let us consider a very simple example. Assume that a research institute is planning to increase the number of languages on its website to reach a larger number of potential students (indicator of effectiveness). Assume also that adding language X yields 100,000 potential new visitors per year at a cost of 5,000 Euros per year, while adding languages Y and Z increase the value of the indicator to 120,000 visitors per year at a cost of 10,000 euros per year. The second alternative is *prima facie* better than the first one, since a larger number of potential visitors can be reached. However, if costs are taken into account, the picture changes completely. In the first option a new student is reached at an average cost of 0.05 euro, while in the second case, the average cost rises to 0.08 euro. Clearly, resources are allocated more cost-effectively in the first than in the second case.

Although CEA is useful to assess the relative efficiency of alternative projects, it is not suitable to establish that a given project guarantees an efficient use of resources *per se*, as in CEA the net benefit is not computed. The impossibility of determining whether the net benefit it is positive or not is the most important shortcoming of CEA as compared to CBA. However, assuming that the result (or the effect) of a project *is* worthwhile, CEA is very useful to identify the alternative that delivers this result at the lowest average cost.

Given the complexity and multidimensionality of language processes, CEA should be applied carefully in order to avoid simplistic conclusions. For example, standard CEA can be enriched with qualitative data. Moreover, the analysis must be structured so that more than a single effect is taken into account. Nevertheless, its internal logic is robust and it provides a strong analytical framework. It is worth stressing again that the main purpose of the analysis is *not* to compute CE ratios as such, but to understand in which direction they change if the scenarios also change.

The assessment of the distributive effects

The assessment of the distributive consequences of alternative policy options is an equally important dimension of evaluation. As pointed out in Section 2, an efficient policy may be rejected if its distributive consequences are deemed too unfair. More generally, as Myles notes (1995: 7) "it is often the case that the efficient policy is highly inequitable whilst the equitable policy would introduce into the economy significant distortions and disincentives. Given this fact, the design of optimal policy can be seen as the process of reaching the correct trade-off between equity and efficiency objectives". Fairness, therefore, also plays a central role in language policy evaluation, as shown by the rapid increase in the number of contributions on this subject.[7]

Assessing fairness means asking who benefits and who loses from the change from D_1 to D_L (or D_H) — or who benefits or loses "more" and who benefits or loses "less". In our case, the key attribute defining a group with respect to others is, in essence, the mother tongue of its members. Note, however, that in the approach we have been developing, we do not construct a measurement for benefits, since we deliberately focus on a single "benefit", namely, effective communication. Hence, the assessment of who gains and who loses is necessarily a partial one.

A possible strategy is to assume that the distributive effects of alternative policies can be assessed through a set of indicators relating to three distinct phases of communication:

1. *access*
2. *process*
3. *outcome*

The idea behind fairness in "access" is that the actors involved in communication can be seen as actors involved in the creation of a common network to make communication possible (let us call it a "common communication network" — CCN). In this perspective, languages are "threads" linking users, which, in turn, are like nodes of a network. A simple example of communication network is that of M persons of different mother tongues linked by a neutral *lingua franca*. Another kind of network is that based on an equal distribution of active and receptive competences; in this case, everyone can speak his/her language because the other members of the network have receptive skills in that language. The distributive consequences of the creation of a CCN are particularly interesting when the medium of communication is a single language that is at the same time the main language of some (but not all) the individuals making up the network. This is the case, for example, of communication occurring between the majority group and minority groups (e.g. monolingual Spanish speakers with respect to speakers of Basque, Catalan and Galician).

Assessing fairness in "access" means checking how the costs of "access" to a CCN are distributed across language groups. Consider a multilingual organisation and assume that in the current situation, the CCN is such that everyone can use his or her language because translation and interpretation services are provided. Assume also that the cost of these services is X and that it is funded by all groups in proportion to their size. What will be the distributive effects of a reduction in the number of working languages? Some agents will no longer have access to the network unless they learn one of the working languages selected, or get language services at their own expense. Assume that these agents choose the second way to be re-connected to the CCN, and for the sake of the example assume also that the costs they now have to bear are larger than the amount corresponding to their previous contribution to X. Those who have not been excluded from the CCN will benefit from this *without* contributing to the extra cost borne by the excluded.

Clearly, fairness in "access" can take different forms according to the communication intent considered (α, β or γ).

Analysing fairness in terms of "process" means focusing on the distributive effects that arise from the very act of communicating. For example, assume that we are dealing with β-communication in the case of an annual international scientific meeting. Assume also that for a given year, the organisers expand the set of languages in which draft papers can be submitted for review. It is likely that, among other things, this policy will increase the "comfort" of several potential speakers. More precisely, the language policy adopted is likely to decrease the "linguistic insecurity" (cf. Francard, 1993, and Bretegnier and Ledegen, 2002) of potential speakers at the conference, since a larger group of them is now allowed to submit draft papers in their language.

It is worth noting that "soft" aspects of communication like that just presented should not be neglected. The analysis of the distributive effects related to the "outcome" of the communication process addresses the following questions: do some linguistic groups communicate more "effectively" than others — where effectiveness is defined as in the preceding section? Do we observe some changes if we move from situation D_1 to D_L (or D_H)? Notice that in this case, the focus is not on "effective" communication in the organisation *as such* (see above), but rather on how "effectiveness" is *distributed between different language groups*. Assume for example that we are dealing with internal α-communication within an international institution, say the United Nations (UN), and that we are comparing two language regimes (used here for the purposes of explanation). The first, say R_1, is an asymmetrical language regime in which everyone may use any of the 6 official languages of the UN, but all interventions are translated only into French. Hence, everyone ought to have good receptive competence in this language. The second, say R_H, is a language regime where everyone may use any of the 6 official languages but everything is interpreted only into Esperanto (or Latin, or any other language which is *not* the native language of any of the participants). In this case, receptive competence in this language is required. All other things being equal, the second language regime can be considered more linguistically diverse since the number of languages is higher. Assume also that the effectiveness indicator α^i_n, say, the inverse of the number of errors, can be expected to be roughly the same for both R_1 and R_H, that is, the loss of information due to interpreting and difficulties in understanding a foreign language (whether French or Esperanto) is equal. Now, it is likely that what *does* change is the distribution of α^i_n across language groups. In particular, we can expect that α^i_n is more equally distributed in regime R_H than R_1. Due to the importance of the "power" dimension in communication, the analysis of the distributive effects of alternative scenarios is particularly important for γ-communication.

Summing up, the approach developed in this section aims at providing a framework for the identification of the channels though which the distribution of resources is affected at different stages of communication, taking account of different communicational intents. Such a framework is necessary if we want to design compensating measures that can restore fairness in communication.

Concluding remarks

In this paper, we present some guidelines for the evaluation of language policies aiming at managing multilingual communication. The evaluation process is carried out along two analytical dimensions, namely, efficiency and fairness. The general framework presented is intended to provide a basis for further research, in particular in the domain of indicator design. 18 possible configurations are possible, by distinguishing between internal and external communication, three main communicational intents, and three possible dimensions for the assessment of distributive effects (2*3*3); for each configuration, a comparison ought to be made between the status quo and "more diverse" and "less diverse" alternatives.

Efficiency concerns the allocative dimension of evaluation. It implies comparing how resources are allocated under different scenarios so as to single out the scenario promising the best allocation. Efficiency by no mean implies uniformity of tastes and practices or, alternatively, simple cost minimisation. On the contrary, efficiency is a concept that makes no sense unless the *preferences* of social actors are duly taken into account. Just as it may be a perfectly rational choice to travel first class from Brussels to Paris by train (if comfort is important enough to justify paying a higher price), by the same token, it is perfectly rational to pay to have "more comfort" in multilingual communication. Efficiency, therefore, should be understood as a relationship between the benefits we are aiming at and the costs we are willing to accept.

In this paper, the notion of "benefit" of linguistic diversity has been interpreted as "effective communication". We have proposed different definitions of what "effective communication" can mean, in order not to limit ourselves to a reductionist view of communication as a mere transmission of messages and languages as simple tools for conveying information. Clearly, the informatory communicational intent (what we have called α-communication) is part of real-life communication but it is not all. Other analytical dimensions, such as, the cooperative or the strategic dimensions, *are* relevant for language diversity management. The definition of α-, β- and γ-communication constitute an attempt to operationalise this idea.

The methodology proposed is based on the concept of indicator. Indicators are meant to be a tool for comparative analysis. Hence, their goal is not to "measure" or "quantify" communication. Rather, the rationale for using indicators is to assess how they change if we move towards a more (respectively, less) diverse linguistic environment, and more specifically towards a more (less) multilingual communication. Cost evaluation should also be approached through comparison. Assessing different ways to manage multilingual communication in terms of their efficiency, therefore, means evaluating the evolution of the relationship between effectiveness and costs indicators.

The main contribution of this paper is to suggest how this relationship could be logically structured. However, applied linguistics can play a key role in the development of indicators of efficiency and fairness. In scientific communication (cf. Ammon, 2001, and Carli and Calaresu, 2007), for example, concepts like the "quality of knowledge", as well as perspectives derived from the sociology of knowledge in distinct linguistic communities, can have major importance for elaborating indicators. Hence, claiming that the most efficient solution for scientific communication is to operate in a single language is a proposition that ought to be closely scrutinised in the light of possible alternatives, taking into account different definitions of what communication is as well as the preferences of the actors involved. However, comparing alternatives is only possible if the comparison is rigorous and consistent, which requires a set of relevant and robust indicators. Including, as we have done here, the cooperative and strategic dimensions in efficiency evaluation increases the crispness of the comparison by adding a larger set of potential effectiveness indicators that do justice of the complexity of language and communication.

The assessment of the distributive effects of language policies is our second key analytical dimension. By distinguishing between fairness in access, process and outcome, we aim at defining a triple locus for the evaluation of fairness in communication. In this perspective, linguistic justice is not only a matter of finding a rule for sharing the costs of what we have called the common communication network. It also implies that other analytical dimensions, such as linguistic insecurity and inequality in outcome, have a role to play when comparing scenarios. The evaluation of fairness in language policy, therefore, is much more about the study of the material and symbolic consequences of linguistic diversity for the people speaking different languages, than a study of its effects on languages themselves.

Notes

1. For simplicity, no distinction is made in this paper between the terms fairness, equity and justice.

2. The concept of linguistic environment can be defined as a theoretical construct that "subsumes in an extensive (but obviously not exhaustive) fashion all the relevant information about the *status*, in the broadest sense of the word, of the various languages present in a given polity at a certain time. This includes the number of speakers, individual proficiency levels in the various languages, the domains of use of each language by different types of actors (individuals, corporations, state, civil society organizations), their attitudes towards the languages considered, etc." (Grin, 1999: 47).

3. A full symmetrical system of interpretation and translation is a system in which all the official languages of a meeting are directly translated into and from each other. The relay technique involves two stages to translate a message from language *A* to language *B*. First *A* is interpreted into language *X*, known as the "pivot" language. Then the message is interpreted from language *X* into language *B*.

4. This list of parameters is involved in the definition of what House and Rehbein call "linguistic constellation". This concept is very close to what we called "linguistic environment" (see footnote 2).

5. The distinction between discourse and text is defined as follows: "whereas the discourse situation is one in which speaker are hearer are co-present and can co-ordinate their speech actions *in situ*, written text is, systematically speaking, distributed over two situations, that of production and that of reception, such that a text must verbalize everything necessary for its reception at some different point in time, possibly by several different (groups of) readers." (House and Rehbein, 2004: 3).

6. For a discussion of the distinction between these two concepts in language policy evaluation, see e.g. Grin (2001). See also Grin and Vaillancourt (1999) and Grin (2001) as an example of how CEA can be applied to language policy evaluation.

7. . See in particular, Pool (1991), Pool (1996), Church and King (1993), de Briey and van Parijs (2002), van Parijs (2004a, 2004b), Grin (1997, 2004a, 2004b, 2005), Fidrmuc *et al.* (2004), Ginsburgh and Weber (2005), Fidrmuc and Ginsburgh (2007), and Gazzola (2006a, 2006b). A review of the debate on linguistic justice among philosophers is provided in de Schutter (2007). See also Kymlicka and Patten (2003).

References

Ammon, U. (ed.) 2001. *The Dominance of English as a Language of Science. Effects on other languages and language communities*. Berlin: Mouton de Gruyter.

Arnsperger, C. & van Parijs, P. 2000. *Ethique économique et sociale*. Paris: La Découverte.

Boadway, R.W. & Bruce, N. 1984. *Welfare Economics*. Oxford: Blackwell.

Boardman, A.E., Greenberg, D.H., Vining, A.R. & Weimer, D.L. 2006. *Cost-Benefit Analysis: Concepts and practice,* 3rd edn. Upper Saddle River NJ: Prentice Hall.

Brent, R. J. 1997. *Applied Cost-Benefit Analysis*. Cheltenham: Edward Elgar.

Bretegnier, A. & Ledegen, G. (eds). 2002 *Sécurité/insécurité linguistique. Terrains et approches diversifiés*, Actes de la 5° Table Ronde du Moufia. Paris: L'Harmattan/A.U.F.

Carey, J.W. 1992. *Communication as Culture: Essays on media and society*. London: Routledge.

Carli, A. & Calaresu, E. 2007. Language and science. In *Handbook of Language and Communication: Diversity and Change*, M. Hellinger & A. Pauwels (eds.), 523–52. Berlin: Mouton de Gruyter.

Charaudeau, P. 1995. Ce que communiquer veut dire. *Sciences humaines* 51: 20–23.

Church, J. & King, I. 1993. Bilingualism and network externalities. *Canadian Journal of Economics* 27(2): 335–45.

de Briey, L. & Van Parijs, P. 2002. La justice linguistique comme justice coopérative. *Revue de philosophie économique* 5: 5–37.

de Schutter, H. 2007 Language policy and political philosophy: On the emerging linguistic justice debate. *Language Problems & Language Planning* 31(1): 1–23.

De Swaan 2001 *Words of the World. The global language system*. Cambridge: Polity Press.

Dunn, W.N. 2004. *Public Policy Analysis: An introduction*, 3rd edn. Upper Saddle River NJ: Prentice Hall.

Fidrmuc, J. & Ginsburgh, V. 2007. Languages in the European Union: The quest for equality and its cost. *European Economic Review* 51 : 1351–1369.

Fidrmuc, J., Ginsburgh, V. & Weber, S. 2004. Le français, deuxième langue de l'Union européenne? *Économie publique* 15(2): 43–63.

Francard, M. (ed.) 1993. L'insécurité linguistique dans les communautés francophones périphériques. *Cahiers de l'Institut de linguistique de Louvain* 19.

Gazzola, M. 2006a. La gestione del multilinguismo nell'Unione europea. In *Le sfide della politica linguistica di oggi: Fra la valorizzazione del multilingualismo migratorio locale e le istanze del plurilinguismo europeo*, A. Carli (ed.), 17–117. Milan: FrancoAngeli.

Gazzola, M. 2006b. Managing multilingualism in the European Union: Language policy evaluation for the European Parliament. *Language Policy* 5(4): 393–417.

Ginsburgh, V. & Weber, S. 2005. Language disenfranchisement in the European Union. *Journal of Common Market Studies* 43(2): 273–86.

Grin, F. 1994. L'identification des bénéfices de l'aménagement linguistique: La langue comme actif naturel. Sociolinguistic Studies and Language Planning — XVI Colloque annuel de l'association de linguistique des provinces atlantiques, Université de Moncton, 67–101.

Grin, F. (ed.) 1996. *Economic Approaches to Language and Language Planning*. Theme issue No. 121 of the *International Journal of the Sociology of Language*.

Grin, F. 1997. Gérer le plurilinguisme européen: approche économique au problème de choix. *Sociolinguistica* 11: 1–15.

Grin, F. 1999. Supply and demand as analytical tools in language. In *Exploring the Economics of Language*, Breton, A. (ed.), 31–62. Ottawa: Canadian Heritage.

Grin, F. 2001. On effectiveness and efficiency in education: Operationalizing the concepts. *Zeitschrift für Pädagogik* 43: 87–97.

Grin, F. 2003. Language planning and economics. *Current Issues in Language Planning* 4(1): 1–66.

Grin, F. 2004a. L'anglais comme *lingua franca*: Questions de coût et d'équité. Commentaire sur l'article de Philippe Van Parijs. *Économie publique* 15(2): 33–41.

Grin, F. 2004b. L'élargissement de l'Union européenne: Questions de coût et justice linguistique. *Panoramiques* 69: 97–104.

Grin, F. 2005. *L'enseignement des langues étrangères comme politique publique.* Rapport au Haut Conseil de l'évaluation de l'école 19.

Grin, F. & Vaillancourt, F. 1997. The economics of multilingualism: Overview and analytical framework. In *Multilingualism and Multilingual Communities,* W. Grabe (ed.), 43–65. Cambridge: CUP.

Grin, F. & Vaillancourt, F. 1999. *The Cost-effectiveness Evaluation of Minority Language Policies: Case studies on Wales, Ireland and the Basque Country.* Flensburg: European Centre for Minority Issues.

House, J. & Rehbein, J. 2004. What is 'multilingual communication'?. In *Multilingual communication,* J. House and J. Rehbein (eds.), 1–18. Amsterdam: John Benjamins.

Jernudd, B. H. 1971. Notes on economics analysis for solving language problems. In *Can Language be Planned?,* J. Rubin & B. Jernudd (eds.), 263–76. Honolulu: The University Press of Hawaii.

Just, R. E., Hueth, D. L. & Schmitz, A. 2004. *The Welfare Economics of Public Policy: A practical approach to project and policy evaluation.* Cheltenham: Edward Elgar.

Kymlicka, W. 2002. *Contemporary Political Philosophy: An introduction,* 2nd edn. Oxford: OUP.

Kymlicka, W. & Patten, A. (eds). 2003. *Language Rights and Political Theory.* Oxford: OUP.

Lamizet, B. & Silem, A. 1997. *Dictionnaire encyclopédique des sciences de l'information et de la communication.* Paris: Ellipses.

Levin, H.M. & MacEwan, P.J. 2001. *Cost-Effectiveness Analysis: Methods and applications,* 2nd ed. Thousand Oaks CA: Sage.

Moulin, H. 2003. *Fair Division and Collective Welfare.* Cambridge MA: The MIT Press.

Mueller, D.C. 2003. *Public Choice III.* Cambridge: CUP.

Mühlhäusler, P. & Damania, R. 2004. Economic costs and benefits of australian indigenous languages. Discussion Paper Prepared for Australian Government Aboriginal and Torres Strait Islander Services (ATSIS), University of Adelaide.

Myles, G.D. 1995. *Public Economics.* Cambridge: CUP.

Patrinos, H.A. & Velez, E. 1995. Costs and benefits of bilingual education in Guatemala. World Bank, HCO Dissemination Notes, Washington.

Paulré, B. 1993. L'organisation entre information et communication. In *Dictionnaire critique de la communication,* L. Sfez (ed.), 519–68. Paris: Presses universitaires de France.

Pool, J. 1991. The official language problem. *American Political Science Review* 25(2): 485–514.

Pool, J. 1996. Optimal language regimes for the European Union. *International Journal of the Sociology of Language* 121: 159–79.

Ricento, T. 2006. Language policy: Theory and practice — An introduction. In *An Introduction to Language Policy: Theory and method,* T. Ricento (ed.), 10–23. Oxford: Blackwell.

Rossi, P.H., Lipsey, M.W. & Freeman, H.E. 2004. *Evaluation: A systematic approach,* 7th edn. Thousand Oaks CA: Sage.

Vaillancourt, F. 1995. Economic costs and benefits of the official languages: Some observations. In *Official Languages and the Economy. New Canadian Perspectives,* Department of Canadian Heritage, 103–18. Ottawa: Canadian Heritage Series.

van Parijs, P. 2004a. Europe's linguistic challenge. *Archives européennes de sociologie* 45(1): 113–54.

van Parijs, P. 2004b. L'anglais comme *lingua franca* de l'Union européenne: Impératif de solidarité, source d'injustice, facteur de déclin? *Économie publique* 15(2): 13–32.

Zajac, E.E. 1995. *Political Economy of Fairness.* Cambridge MA: The MIT Press.

Authors' address

École de traduction et d'interprétation
Université de Genève — Suisse
40, Bd du Pont-d'Arve
CH-1211 Genève

michele.gazzola@eti.unige.ch; francois.grin@eti.unige.it

Shift in language policy in Malaysia
Unravelling reasons for change, conflict and compromise in mother-tongue education

Saran Kaur Gill
Universiti Kebangsaan, Malaysia

Malaysia experienced a major shift in language policy in 2003 for the subjects of science and maths. This meant a change in the language of education for both national and national-type schools. For national schools, this resulted in a shift from Bahasa Malaysia, the national language to English. Parallel with this, to ensure homogeneity of impact of change, the State persuaded the national-type schools, which have been utilizing the language of community, Mandarin and Tamil respectively, as medium of instruction since independence in 1957, to shift to English for the teaching of science and maths.

This paper aims to unravel the socio-political reasons underlying the shift with a focus on the Chinese community's responses to the change. This will be carried out by examining the discourses of the debate contested by members of the Chinese community, juxtaposed against the reasons for the change, set forth by the State, as articulated by the former Prime Minister of Malaysia, Mahathir Mohamad. This multi-pronged approach will be used to unravel the underlying ideologies for the change and the reluctant compromise that was reached by the Chinese community.

Introduction

Malaysia experienced a major shift in language policy in 2003 for the subjects of science and mathematics. This meant a change in the language of education for both national and national-type schools. National schools are schools that use Bahasa Malaysia, the mother-tongue of the dominant ethnic group and Malaysia's national language, as the medium of instruction. On the other hand, the national-type concept gave the schools the right to teach in the language of their choice, using the mother-tongue of minority communities as medium of instruction, for example, Mandarin and Tamil medium schools. At the same time, for national-type schools the national language, Bahasa Malaysia, is a compulsory school subject (Asmah 1987: 60). For national schools, the

AILA Review 20 (2007), **106–122**. DOI 10.1075/aila.20.09gil
ISSN 1461–0213 / E-ISSN 1570–5595 © John Benjamins Publishing Company

recent change in language policy resulted in a shift from Bahasa Malaysia to English. Parallel with this, to ensure homogeneity of impact of change, the State persuaded the national-type schools, which have been utilizing the language of community, Mandarin and Tamil respectively, as medium of instruction since independence in 1957, to shift to English for the teaching of science and mathematics.

There are many other ethnic communities in Malaysia but due to exigencies of space it will only be the Chinese community that will be focused on. Malaysia has a population of 25 million. The Chinese community makes up 26% of the population, numbering 6,500,000. The dominant ethnic group, the Malays, make up 65.1% of the population, numbering 16,275,000. The other significant minority group — the Tamil community makes up 7.7% (1,925,000) of the population (http://www.statistics.gov. my, Census 2000). In addition, there are a host of other smaller minority groups.

The Chinese community's response to the required change will be carried out by examining the discourses of the debate contested by members of the Chinese community. These contestations will be juxtaposed against the reasons for the change set forth by the State as articulated by the former Prime Minister of Malaysia, Mahathir Mohamad. This multi-pronged approach will be used to unravel the underlying ideologies, that is, the set of beliefs that underpin the political systems in the country and that influence decision-making re: language policy in Malaysia.

At the start, it will be pertinent to establish the link between politics and language policy to enable us to unravel the socio-political reasons and ideology underlying the shift in language policy.

Language policy and politics

Research in the field of language policy of the 50's, 60's and 70's when many developing nations attained their independence, focused on the traditional mainstay of examining language as a mode for problem-solving and development. This was the period when ethno-nationalism was of prime concern and there was a strong need to establish a common language as a unifying force to draw multi-ethnic groups together. Tollefson criticizes the work of this period as failing "to capture the complex social and political context of language policies," and accepting "uncritically the claims of state authorities" (Tollefson 2002: 4).

Gradually, there developed a strong feeling amongst those in the language policy and planning field that there was a need to understand the reasons for the decisions made on language status and use in the various countries. This led to the field of critical language policy and planning (see Tollefson 2006: 42–59, for a delineation of this field). One of the dominant strands emerging from this field is that of the inextricable link between language — especially language policies in education — with economic, political, socio-cultural complexities and more recently the science and technology ideology.

Tsui and Tollefson highlight this as they discuss research in the field of medium-of-instruction policy. They draw our attention to the fact that decisions on choice of language in education should not just be looked at superficially but need to be examined in greater depth for us to unearth and understand the reasons for decisions that have been made. They stress the fact that

> [a]ll too often, policy makers put forward an educational agenda that justifies policy decisions regarding the use and / or the prohibition of a particular language or languages. Yet, behind the educational agenda are political, social and economic agendas that serve to protect the interests of particular political and social groups. The tension between these agendas is difficult to resolve, and almost invariably leads to the triumph of the political, social or economic agenda over the educational agenda. For this reason, we feel that it is important, when examining medium-of-instruction policy issues, to ask and address the questions, "Which Agenda? Whose Agenda?" (Tsui and Tollefson 2004: 2).

It is in this context of asking these questions that this paper is approached. These questions will drive the examination of the reasons for the shift in language policy leading onto the resultant conflict and the compromises negotiated by the Chinese community for political stability. We now move on to setting the context for the shift in language policy.

Context for change in language policy

On the 11th May 2002, a drastic and sudden change in the medium of instruction was announced in the mass media (Mahathir Mohamad, New Straits Times, 11 May 2002:1). This coincided with the fact that the former Prime Minister was to step down from office on the 31 October 2003, a time lapse of 17 months and 20 days to be exact. Critics say he had the courage to carry through this change in language of instruction because he had nothing to lose politically since he was stepping down from office.

This then raises the question of whether a man who has led the nation for the past 22 years and taken it to such heights, initiate a major change in language of instruction that would disadvantage the nation and its people? Would it not be pertinent instead to examine and try to understand the factors that provided the impetus for this change? This then led to an interview with Mahathir Mohamad. It was relevant to access directly the reasons that caused him to initiate this shift in policy. The interview took place on the 16, June 2005 and the data from this interview will help unravel the State's stand regarding the change in language policy, reflected through his voice.

The first question at the interview focused on the reasons for the change in language policy. Mahathir was asked, with regards to the recent change in the medium-of-instruction in schools, which now have impacted higher education, what were the reasons that provided the impetus for this change in language policy for the fields of science and maths? He said:

> Education is for the purpose of acquiring knowledge. The most important thing is the acquisition of knowledge. If you have to use a language which makes the knowledge more easily accessible, you should use that language. Historically, the Europeans learnt Arabic in order to access the knowledge of the Arabs [...] but because of their work they also learnt Greek in order to access the language and knowledge [...] so if you want knowledge you have to acquire the language in which the knowledge is available.
>
> Our education system is like any other education system. It's meant to enable us to acquire knowledge. If we have the knowledge available in the national language, by all means, go ahead but the fact is that in science the research that is being done is moving at a very fast pace. Everyday literally thousands of papers on new research are being published and practically all of them are in English. To translate English into Bahasa, would require a person with 3 skills. Skill in the 2 languages and skill in the subject that is to be translated and we don't have very many people who are qualified to do that or who wish to do that. That is why it is easier if you learn English and the students can have direct access to all the knowledge that is available in English (Interview conducted by Gill, 16 June, 2005).

The above draws in the issue of translation and the struggles of the national language to keep up with the proliferation of knowledge in English. If we refer to the past development of Bahasa Malaysia, it will be noticed that, like many other languages in the developing world, it underwent a period of modernization to equip it with corpus to develop as a language of knowledge for the field of science and technology. Together with these efforts, huge resources were injected into the development of the language and its utilization for the field of science and technology. These included translation efforts and encouragement of academic writings in Bahasa Malaysia. All of these extended over a period of thirty years. Despite all these efforts, Bahasa Malaysia, like many other languages, found it an uphill challenge to keep up with knowledge proliferation in English. This then highlights one of the major reasons for the change, which is the inability of translation and writings in Bahasa Malaysia to keep pace with the proliferation of knowledge in the field of science and technology in English. This is explicated in detail in Gill (in press).

One common comment to the above is "why couldn't the students cope with publications in English?" They could still be taught in Bahasa Malaysia and have their references in English — a bilingual situation that is found in many other parts of the world. Nambiar (2005) explains this when she concludes that for learners who are less proficient, (which many students are in the public university context), understanding a text is more a language problem than a reading problem. It is generally assumed that if a learner can read in Bahasa Malaysia he can also read in English. It is erroneous to make this assumption because the reality is that if a learner has a low level of proficiency in English, he/she will find it challenging to process a text in that language. This is magnified when learners have to deal with scientific and technical texts where they have to struggle with both academic content knowledge and linguistic knowledge. This is because when texts become more conceptually complex, and there is minimum support linguistically because of poor proficiency, then this problem is exacerbated. Therefore, regardless of which language they use, if their proficiency is weak, then their processing and comprehension skills suffer.

Given this problematic situation, to ensure access to knowledge and information in English, there developed tremendous reliance on translated material from English to Bahasa Malaysia and to writings in Bahasa Malaysia. But as explained by Mahathir in interview with Gill (2005) and further elaborated on in Gill (in press), these processes were not able to keep pace with the proliferation of knowledge in English.

The weak competency levels in English have led to another problem. This is related to the fact that the national education policy has produced monolinguals, graduates fluent mainly in Bahasa Malaysia. Instead, presently, what is needed especially in this age of the knowledge economy and international competition are effective bilinguals, fluent in both Bahasa Malaysia and English, to cope with the demands of the private sector workplace. This is a situation exacerbated by the bifurcation of higher education. This is discussed in detail in Gill (2002) and will be summarized here. The bifurcation of higher education led to public universities which used Bahasa Malaysia and private universities which, through the liberalization of higher education, were able to use English as the language of education. The graduates from the private universities, because of their fluency in English and the marketability of their courses, were in greater demand in the private sector which was gradually becoming the main employer of graduates from universities. This gave them a distinct advantage over those from the public universities in vying for jobs in this sector. The linguistic disadvantage of graduates from public universities has resulted in large numbers (approximately 24,728) who have not been able to obtain jobs in the private sector. Mustapha Mohamad, presently the Minister of Higher Education and formerly the executive director of the government sponsored National Economic Action Council (NEAC), articulated the reasons for this problem clearly. He said:

> This is basically a Malay problem as 94 per cent of those registered with the Government are bumiputeras (sons of the soil), Chinese constitute 3.7 per cent and Indians, 1.6 per cent. It has to do with the courses taken, and …. Also their poor performance in and command of the English language (New Straits Times, 14 March, 2002: 1 & 12).

These macro reasons resulted in a change in language of education, from Bahasa Malaysia to English in the education system of national schools in a staggered fashion — beginning with Primary One, Secondary One and Lower Six. This took place within a period of six months from the timing of the announcement to implementation in the school system.

Parallel with this, to ensure homogeneity of impact of change, the State persuaded the national-type schools, which have been utilizing the language of community, Mandarin and Tamil respectively, as medium of instruction since independence in 1957, to shift to English for the teaching of science and mathematics. This then takes us to the second part of the paper which explores the responses of the Chinese community to this directive for change and the resultant conflict and mode of compromise.

Education in Mandarin and the Chinese community's response to the change: Brief history

History very often provides a reliable window on the events in the past that have led to present systems of education. It is crucial to appreciate these past events to understand responses in present times regarding the change in language of education.

During the period of colonisation, the schooling systems in the Chinese and Tamil medium of education were set up largely because of indifference on the part of the British. This was mainly because the British felt that since the immigrants were regarded as birds of passage who would return to their countries of origin after they had accumulated sufficient wealth, they were not inclined to expend money on the Chinese and Indian vernacular systems of education. As a result, the immigrant communities had to see to the education of their own communities and they were given great freedom to develop their own educational systems. The immigrants spoke their own languages, financed their own schools and designed their own curriculum (Chai 1977: 252).

With this freedom and flexibility afforded to them, the immigrant communities, especially the Chinese community, sowed the seeds for an extensive development of Chinese medium education in what was then known as Malaya. Kua traces the historical development of Chinese medium education when he states that:

> [t]he first Chinese school in the peninsula dates as far back as 1815. As Chinese settlements in Malaya grew, so did the number of Chinese-medium schools. [...] By the 20th century, the independence of the Chinese school system was already established. Its reliance on the Chinese community itself went beyond financial autonomy since the British colonial authorities were so impressed by the high level of communal organization among Malayan Chinese that they left them virtually alone to manage their own affairs. This struggle to preserve and promote the language, education and culture of the Chinese in Malaya involved the active mobilization of the whole Chinese community through the guilds and associations (Kua 1999: 2).

All of this was being developed against the backdrop of Malaysia's language policy, which on closer examination reveals a paradoxical nature. An analysis of the language policy journey since independence till now, a period of over 30 years, fluctuates between both recognition and provision for linguistic pluralism and in contrast, periods

of establishing the primacy of linguistic assimilation with the establishment of various educational acts to facilitate this. It is the latter approach of the nation's language
policy that has led to frustration amongst the proponents of mother-tongue education
in Malaysia.

Linguistic pluralism

In the years of newly attained independence, the liberal educational policies that supported linguistic pluralism provided the environment for the development of the largest number of Chinese medium schools in Malaysia outside of mainland China — no
other country has this. This largely has been due to the benevolent and equitable policy
instituted by our Prime Minister at the time of independence, Tunku Abdul Rahman.

One has to refer to the legacy left by him to understand how he recognised the
need for mother tongue language and identity for the various ethnic groups in the
country. We will begin with an examination of post-independence history, which provides an explanation for this liberal policy. After independence, the government of
Malaya came up with the Education Ordinance 1957 which was based on the Razak report (a report by a committee that was formed in 1955 to review the education system
and to make recommendations for an education system best suited for an independent
Malaysia) (Asmah 1979: 14). One of the provisions in the Razak report proved to be
beneficial for the development of mother tongue education and vernacular schools.
Provision S3 of the 1957 Ordinance stated that

> the educational policy of the Federation is to establish a national system of educa-
> tion acceptable to the people as a whole which will satisfy their needs and promote
> their cultural, social, economic and political development as a nation, with the in-
> tention of making the Malay language the national language of the country whilst
> preserving and sustaining the growth of the language and culture of peoples other
> than Malays living in the country (Education Ordinance, No. 2 of 1957: 34&35).

It goes on to state that

> regard shall be had to the general principle that, so far as is compatible with the
> educational policy of the Federation, the provision of efficient instruction and the
> avoidance of unreasonable public expenditure, pupils are to be educated in accor-
> dance with the wishes of their parents (Education Ordinance, No. 2 of 1957: 35).

All of this was part of "drawing up the various policies which all aimed at evolving Malaya, now Malaysia, into an integrated nation" (Asmah 1987: 59) after gaining independence from the British colonial powers. Therefore, the 1956 Razak Report provided for
mother-tongue education at the primary school level to be integrated into the national
education system. This was later legislated into the Education Ordinance 1957. This

resulted in the dominant minority communities, like the Chinese and Tamils, setting up what were described as national-type schools as compared to national schools.

The provision of mother-tongue education in Malaysia began with Stage 4 of Fishman's "Graded Intergenerational Disruption Scale" (see Fishman 1991: 81–121). There are 8 stages in this scale ranging from Stage 1 which is "the most secure position for a minority language" where there is "some use of the minority language (henceforth ML) in higher level educational, occupational, governmental and media realms" to that of the least secure stage, Stage 8, where "remaining speakers of a ML are old and usually vestigial users" (paraphrased in May, 2001: 2). Stage 4 is at the mid-level where the minority language has a functional role to play in the educational system and is used as a medium of instruction.

This is a reasonable provision for an immigrant population as it provides the balance that needs to be maintained between minority community needs and the needs of the state dominated by a majority ethnic group. This is a crucial consideration for ethnic and political stability of most multi-ethnic nations.

Move towards linguistic illiberalism

In the latter post-independence period, the language policies of the nation gradually changed as the needs of the country altered. These were the needs of establishing a national identity amongst the multi-ethnic population. One of the means by which this was facilitated was via the selection and institution of Bahasa Malaysia as the national and official language. This meant that this was the language to be used as medium of instruction at all levels of public education, ranging from the school system to the universities and in public administration. The establishment and acceptance of Bahasa Malaysia in Malaysia's multi-ethnic population was an ongoing struggle for the nation. This was because of Malaysia's colonial past during which English had established itself as the dominant language of education and officialdom. Any language that is trying to assert itself in competition with English, an established international language with economic capital, faces many trials and tribulations. For the dominant ethnic group, for whom Bahasa Malaysia was their mother tongue, it was essential for them to ensure the success of the implementation of Bahasa Malaysia as national and official language as it additionally provided them with a means to legitimise and elevate their presence in this multi-ethnic national domain.

In this phase of linguistic illiberalism, the marginalisation of mother-tongue education began with the Rahman Talib Committee 1960. The recommendations of this Report reversed the liberal approach taken in the Razak Report 1956. Its recommendations were translated into the Education Act 1961. It did this by leaving out crucial aspects of the 1957 Ordinance, as underlined below:

3. The educational policy of the Federation is to establish a national system of education <u>acceptable to the people as a whole</u> which will satisfy their needs and promote their cultural, social, economic and political development as a nation, with the intention of making the Malay language the national language of the country <u>whilst preserving and sustaining the growth of the language and culture of peoples other than Malays living in the country</u> (cited in Yang 1998: 40).

As stated earlier, this is because during this period, Malaysia, focused, like a number of other countries, on the essential "educational agendas of nation-building, national identity and unity …." (Tollefson and Tsui 2004: viii). This is supported by Asmah, who states unequivocally that

> the national language is the basis for the identification of the nation as one which is defined by linguistic and cultural characteristic peculiar to itself and which set it apart from others. This is especially so in a multiracial and multilingual indepen- dent country where if a common culture is to unify the young nation, it must have a common language, the national language (Asmah 1982: 19).

The authorities were very serious about "the progressive development of an educa- tional system in which the national language is the main medium of instruction," (para 3 of the Preamble of the Act). As a result, significant resources were channeled to enhancing the status and functional use of Bahasa Malaysia in the education system. Consequently, there was a reduction in the budgets for the upkeep of schools that used the vernacular as the medium of education.

The concerns of the Chinese community towards these changes in the Education Acts have been discussed in detail by Yang in his article, "Constitutional and Legal Provision for Mother Tongue Education in Malaysia." The main thrust of the article is criticism and anxiety towards the various acts culminating in the 1996 Education Act which he says, "does not guarantee the permanent or continued use of mother tongue as the main medium of instruction in the existing national-type primary schools" (Yang 1998: 53).

In the face of these challenging problems, Kua (1999), a leading proponent of mother-tongue education, in his book, "A Protean Saga: The Chinese Schools in Ma- laysia" comprehensively describes the historical struggles of Chinese schools in Malay- sia. He dramatically describes the situation when he says:

> Reviewing its history, one realizes the fact that the Chinese schools system has come about only through blood, sweat, tears and sheer political will of the Chi- nese community in this country to defend their mother-tongue education … truly, a protean saga (Kua 1999: 2).

Despite these challenges, there are presently 1,280 Chinese-medium primary schools and 60 Independent Chinese Secondary Schools in the country. This is an amazing fact given that their establishment, maintenance and sustenance has been largely com- munity driven from the nineteenth century to now.

In these present times, this raises one of the major challenges facing the national-type schools in the country — this is the implementation of change in medium of instruction from Mandarin to English for science and mathematics. It is important to investigate this because any change in language policy can only be successful if the agents on the ground can be convinced as to the efficacy of the change.

The response to change of MOI in Chinese schools

As stated earlier, in Malaysia, a sudden change in the medium of instruction was announced in the mass media on the 11th of May 2002" (Mahathir Mohamad, New Straits Times, 11 May 2002:1). This led to a reinstitution of English as the medium of instruction for science and mathematics in the education system in a staggered fashion — beginning with Primary One, Secondary One and Lower Six.

Chinese educationists' response to the implementation of change in medium of instruction

The Chinese school community was very unhappy with the change in the medium of instruction from Mandarin to English. Khoo Kay Peng, Executive Director of Sedar Institute, which is the think-tank of Gerakan, one of the multi-racial political parties in Malaysia, quotes from a number of studies to build up the integral case for mother-tongue education. He says:

> Studies conducted at George Mason University in Virginia since 1985 have shown that children do better if they get a basic education in their own language. It positively established a direct link between academic results and the time spent learning in the mother tongue. Children who come to school with a solid foundation in their mother tongue develop stronger literacy abilities in school language. Children develop concepts and thinking skills faster in their own mother tongue because the majority of children's early childhood is exposed primarily to their own mother tongue. This is also the case for Malaysia; with the exception of urbanites with access to additional educational support services and facilities for their children (Khoo, accessed from MCA website on October 10, 2005).

His argument is that children through their strong literacy skills access knowledge and information better in their mother-tongue.

Chinese educators felt aggrieved that despite the fact that students in Chinese medium education outperformed students in national schools in the field of science and mathematics, they had to change their medium of instruction. They just could not understand any reason for the need to change, other than the government wanting to change the identity of the national-type schools. Dr. Kua, the principal of New Era

College, a tertiary level institution that uses Mandarin as the language of education, expresses the community's concerns when he says:

> ... the Chinese ... education lobbies ... see the teaching of Maths and Science in English as a serious threat to the existence of the mother-tongue education system because at a stroke, it homogenizes all the primary schools. There would be no need for Chinese ... schools when the schools become effectively English schools with a subject in Malay or Chinese (Kua 2005: 175).

Placing this in context will provide a clearer picture of the Chinese community's concerns. At the UPSR level (this is the level of Primary 6 where students have their first public exam), with this change, the subjects will be English, Mandarin, Bahasa Malaysia, Maths in English and Science in English. This means that if they implement the policy as it is being done in national schools, then everything will be in English except for Mandarin and Bahasa Malaysia — both language subjects. Therefore this erases the Chinese make up of these schools and transforms them into English medium schools with Mandarin and Bahasa Malaysia offered as language subjects.

The Chinese educationists were extremely unhappy with this situation. But despite their frustrations, this language policy was a "top-down" policy. This meant that these were "policies that come from people of power and authority to make decisions for a certain group, without consulting the end-users of the language" (Kaplan & Baldauf 1997: 196). Therefore given that it was not possible to avert the directive, they sought to influence the mode of implementation. Their reluctance was reflected in a document drafted by the Malaysian Chinese Association (MCA) Central Committee, (MCA is the main Chinese political party in the country), in which they stress that "an important principle firmly upheld by MCA is that the teaching of mathematics and science in the Chinese primary schools should mainly be in the mother tongue" (MCA 9 Point Party Platform: 30). Underpinning all of this was the strong need to maintain their Chinese identity manifest through mother-tongue education. They suggested a 222 formula for implementation of the teaching of science and mathematics in English, which would have had a minimal impact on the use of Mandarin for the teaching of science and mathematics.

The 222 formula means 2 hours for maths, science and English respectively. In terms of implementation, it means for maths, out of 10 teaching hours a week, 2 hours will be conducted in English and 8 hours in Mandarin. For science, out of 6 teaching hours a week, 2 hours will be conducted in English and 8 hours in Mandarin. 2 hours a week will be allotted to English.

		English	Mandarin
English		2	
Maths	10 hrs per week	2	8
Science	6 hours per week	2	4

The former president of the Malaysian Chinese Association, Ling Liong Sik, took these recommendations to the former Prime Minister of Malaysia, Mahathir Mohamad, for negotiation. Datar, a political scientist, describes this mode of negotiation as

> a unique consensus between the leaders of the Malays, Chinese and Indians — important decisions affecting the communities would be worked out as a process of compromise at top level closed door meetings instead of being subjected to the process of democratic debate at the grassroots level. Instead of negating the ethnic configuration, it accepted its primacy and worked within the political framework (Datar 1983: 14).

After the negotiations behind closed doors, the leader of the Malaysian Chinese party, who attended the meeting with the community recommendation of a 222 formula, returned instead with the 243 formula which provided more hours for the teaching of science and mathematics in English.

243 Formula

This meant that for mathematics, out of 10 teaching hours, 4 hours will be in English and 6 hours in Mandarin. For science, out of 6 teaching hours, 3 hours will be in English and 3 hours in Mandarin. 2 hours a week will be allotted to English.

Lower Primary — Std. 1–3 2002–2003

		English	Mandarin
English	0 hours per week	2	
Maths	10 hours per week	4	6
Science	6 hours per week	3	3

Many Chinese educationists were unhappy with this outcome and politically did not look upon it favourably. They wanted as much as possible to minimize the role of English in their education systems. It was rumored through the grapevine that this was one of the contributory factors that led to the Chinese political leader stepping down from a long-standing career in politics.

Soon after this was settled, another dilemma arose. This was because the first batch of students who were in lower primary (Primary 1–3), beginning with Primary one in 2003, leading onto Primary 3 in 2005, had moved to Upper Primary (Primary 4–6) in 2006.

If the 243 formula were to be applied to the upper primary distribution of time for science and mathematics, it would have meant greater time for English and lesser for Mandarin. It must also be borne in mind that the time allocated for English was doubled from the 2 hours per week for the lower primary level to 4 hours a week for the upper primary level. Maths now has an allocation of 7 hours per week. With the

243 formula, as depicted in the table below, this has meant 4 hours for Maths in English and 3 hours for Maths in Mandarin. For science, for a 6 hours allocation per week, this has meant 3 hours for science in English and 3 hours for science in Mandarin.

243 Formula for Upper Primary Levels

		English	Mandarin
English	2 hours per week	4 (doubled)	
Maths	7 hours per week	4	3
Science	6 hours per week	3	3

The Chinese educationists' point of contention was: How can there be less Mandarin and more English? These schools will not be Chinese schools anymore. Therefore discussions and negotiations had to take place in 2005 and the Chinese educationists met with the Education Minister, Hishamuddin Hussein.

They told him that the 243 formula would not be able to work at the Upper Primary level. The solution recommended then was a 6232 Formula.

6232 Formula for Upper Primary Levels

		English	Mandarin
English	4 hours per week	4	
Maths	7 increases to 8 hours per week	2	6
Science	5 hours per week	2	3

For this to be applied, maths had to be increased from 7 to 8 hours per week. For this 8 hours of maths, 2 hours were to be taught in English and 6 hours in Mandarin. The allocation for Science was reduced from 6 hours to 5 hours a week. Out of this 5 hours, 2 hours would be taught in English and 3 hours in Mandarin.

This formula maintains the dominance of Chinese as a medium of instruction. But there were concerns that the 5 hours per week for science might not be sufficient to cover the syllabus. Therefore, they might have to have extra hours/classes to ensure that there is sufficient time for the subject.

Whither the way forward?

Where then do we go from here? How does one reconcile the divergent stands? What is the political agenda behind all of these initiatives?

In an interview with a leading proponent of Chinese language education, he says in reply to the above question that

> [f]rom a very cynical suspicious mind of somebody who has written about Chinese education, this change in medium of instruction is an effective way of changing the character of Chinese and Tamil schools in one fell swoop and you would have accomplished the ultimate objective of converting all Chinese and Tamil schools into national schools (interview conducted on 20th July 2006).

Therefore, you have on one hand, the group that is striving for the maintenance of ethnic identity as reflected through mother-tongue education. On the other hand, you have forces that would like to see more linguistic and educational commonality at the national level that cuts across the various ethnic groups in the country.

Schmidt describes these two groups as the "advocates for minority language equality ... (who) speak in the language of justice, while proponents of national unity speak in terms of national good." Therefore, this results in one of the most challenging complexities of language policy conflict, which is that "its partisans often appear to be speaking past each other — participating in parallel discourse — rather than to each other, seemingly motivated by differing concerns" (2000: 42). Tsui and Tollefson stress a similar point in their book "Medium of Instruction Policies: Which Agenda? Whose Agenda?" when they reiterate that "[t]he tension between these agendas is difficult to resolve, and almost invariably leads to the triumph of the political, social or economic agenda over the educational agenda" (Tsui & Tollefson 2004: 2).

Therefore just as national schools have shifted from Bahasa, the national language and more importantly, the mother tongue of the dominant ethnic group, to English for science and maths for political reasons, it was necessary that the national-type schools, which use the mother tongue of the minority groups, do the same as well.

This is not surprising because it is a common fact, that in any nation that is multi-ethnic, made up of a dominant indigenous ethnic community and other less highly populated ethnic communities, it is essential for the overall stability of the country that the dominant group feels secure and stays educationally and economically on par with the rest. It is in this context, that Mahathir emphasizes the need to develop and establish ourselves as a people first, using whatever language we need to do this, before we can ensure that our language receives the recognition that it deserves. He says:

> We need to move from the extreme form of nationalism which concentrates on being a language nationalist only, not a knowledge nationalist, not a development oriented nationalist. I feel that we should be a development oriented nationalist. We want our people to succeed, to be able to stand tall, to be respected by the rest of the world. Not to be people with no knowledge of science and technology, very poor, very backwards, working as servants to other people. If we have no knowledge we will be servants to those with knowledge (Interviewed by Gill, 16 June 2005).

Mahathir's ideology is very closely linked to the human capital theory, as explicated by Grin when he regards language attributes, in this case English, as assets, comparable to education in general or more specifically computer literacy (Grin 1999: 9). Through this approach, linguistic assets provide the thrust for local knowledge creation and development, which in turn enhances a people's stature and prestige in both the national and world communities. This is a challenge that takes place over time but this is the reality of one of the main reasons underpinning the change in language of education.

Conclusion

In conclusion, attention should be drawn to the fact the Government is very concerned about ensuring that the majority of Malaysians study in national schools so that they have the multi-ethnic environment in which to study and play together, to grow up together and progress together. This is essential for the development of national integration and national unity. This concern attains an even greater significance when the reality is that close to 80% of Chinese parents send their children to the national-type Mandarin schools, at the primary level at least, schools that are largely mono-ethnic in composition.

In relation to the above concern, findings from an interview conducted with a leader of the think-tank of a Chinese political party presents the following viewpoint:

> if the government improves the quality of their national schools and builds up the multi-racial composition of teaching staff and the management of these schools then more Chinese parents would be inclined to send their children to national schools" (interview conducted on the 5 July 2006).

Dr. Raja Nazrin Shah, a respected member of the Perak State royal family, stresses the same point when he says

> there should be a concerted effort to make national schools the preferred learning institutions.... 80 per cent of the teachers at the school were Malays. This, he said, did not reflect the country's multi-racial population and neither was it an indication of the actual population ratio (Mimi Syed Yusof in New Sunday Times, August 13, 2006: 19).

With this change in the make up of national schools, it is estimated that "at least 30–40% of children who are presently in Chinese medium schools would be sent to national schools by their parents" (Interview conducted on the 5 July 2006 with leader of Chinese political party think-tank).

It is this that the government is trying its best to do under the leadership of our present Minister of Education, Hishamuddin Hussein. It will not be politically feasible to eliminate Chinese-medium schools — this will lead to political chaos and instability for the nation. Instead, the Minister of Education is working hard at efforts to make our national schools the schools of choice so that they will reflect the multi-ethnicity of the nation and provide for plural integration. In the national school system, plurality of ethnic identity is recognized through the provision of mother-tongue languages as subjects whilst there is integration into the national milieu through the national system of education with most subjects still in Bahasa Malaysia, the national language and science and mathematics in English. It is this pluralistic approach that will lead the way forward for our Malaysian nation so that we deal not with Whose agenda? And Which agenda? but instead work interdependently towards a common Malaysian agenda.

References

Asmah, H.O. 1979. *Language Planning for Unity and Efficiency. A study of the language status and corpus planning of Malaysia*. Kuala Lumpur: Dewan Bahasa dan Pustaka.

Asmah, H.O. 1987. *Malay in its Sociocultural Context*. Kuala Lumpur: Dewan Bahasa dan Pustaka

Asmah, H.O. 1982. *Language and Society in Malaysia*. Kuala Lumpur: Dewan Bahasa dan Pustaka.

Chai, H.C. 1977. *Education and Nation Building in Plural Societies. The West Malaysian experience*. Canberra: Australian National University Press.

Datar, K.K. 1983. *Malaysia Quest for a Politics of Consensus*. Delhi: Vikas Press.

Education Ordinance 1957.

Fishman, J.A. 1991. *Reversing Language Shift*. Clevedon: Multilingual Matters.

Gill, S.K. 2002. *International Communication: English language challenges for Malaysia*. Serdang: Universiti Putra Malaysia Press.

Gill, S.K. 2005. Interview with Tun Dr. Mahathir Mohamad, the former Prime Minister of Malaysia on 16 June at the Petronas Twin Towers, Kuala Lumpur, Malaysia.

Gill, S.K. 2005. Language policy in Malaysia: Reversing direction. *Language Policy* 4(3): 241–260.

Gill, S. K. In press. Contrasting language policy changes in higher education in Malaysia. In *Language Issues in English-Medium Universities Across Asia*, N. Bruce & C. Davison (eds). Hong Kong: Hong Kong University Press.

Grin, F. 1999. Economics. In *Handbook of Language and Ethnic Identity*, J.A. Fishman (ed.), 9–24. New York NY: OUP.

Kaplan, R.B. & Baldauf, R.B. 1997. *Language Planning from Practice to Theory*. Clevedon: Multilingual Matters.

Khoo, K. P. 10th October 2005. Creating unnecessary disagreements over agreements. Accessed on www.mca.org.my.

Kua, K.S. 1999. *A Protean Saga. The Chinese schools of Malaysia,* 3rd edn. Kajang: Dong Jiao Zong Higher Learning Centre.

Mahathir M. *New Straits Times*, 11 May 2002:1.

May, S. 2001. *Language and Minority Rights. Ethnicity, nationalism and the politics of language*. Edinburgh: Pearson.

MCA 9 Point Party Platform. January 6, 2006. Kuala Lumpur: Malaysian Chinese Association.

Mimi S.Y. August 13, 2006. National schools must reflect diversity. In *New Sunday Times*: 19.

Mustapha M. March 14, 2002. NEAC: Institutions must ensure graduates are employable. *New Straits Times* 1&2.

Nambiar, R. 2005. Language Learning and Language Use Strategies for Academic Literacy: Towards a theoretical and pedagogical model of language learning. PhD dissertation. Universiti Kebangsaan Malaysia. Bangi

Schmidt, R.S. 2000. Language Policy and Identity Politics in the United States. Philadelphia: Temple University Press.

Tollefson, J.W. 2002. Introduction: Critical issues in educational language policy. In *Language Policies in Education. Critical issues*, J.W. Tollefson (ed.), 3–15. Mahwah NJ: Lawrence Erlbaum.

Tollefson, J.W. 2006. Critical theory in language policy. In *An Introduction to Language Policy. Theory and method*, T. Ricento (ed.), 42–59. Malden MA: Blackwell.

Tollefson, J.W. & Tsui, A.B.M. 2004. Preface. In *Medium of Instruction Policies. Which agenda? Whose agenda?* J.W. Tollefson & A.B.M. Tsui (eds), vii–ix. Mahwah NJ: Lawrence Erlbaum.

Wright, S. 2004. *Language Policy and Language Planning. From nationalism to globalisation*. Basingstoke: Palgrave.

Yang, P.K. 1998. Constitutional & legal education for mother tongue education. In *Mother Tongue Education of Malaysian Ethnic Minorities*, K.S. Kua (ed.), 26–71. Kajang: Dong Jiao Zong Higher Learning Centre.

Author's address

School of Language Studies and Linguistics
Faculty of Social Sciences and Humanities
Universiti Kebangsaan Malaysia
43600 Bangi, Selangor
Malaysia

saran@ukm.my

Global scientific communication
Open questions and policy suggestions

Ulrich Ammon
Universität Duisburg-Essen, Germany

1. The purpose of this concluding discussion

This volume is about the role of different languages in science and scientific communication, with the focus on the status and function of entire languages like English, Chinese, Russian, etc. and not on structural details of these languages — following the distinction between status and corpus in language planning. However, the latter, i.e. corpus issues (language structure, vocabulary, and rules of pragmatics and discourse), on which the study of languages for special purposes would focus, cannot be entirely ignored as questions of modernization and of terminological and pragmatic adequacy of languages for scientific communication arise in this volume, but have not been dealt with in any detail.

This concluding discussion of the issues raised in this volume tries to make some generalizations, without going into a lot of specific details:

– What we have come to know about the topic, i.e. what is reasonably safe knowledge;
– Which questions still need closer scrutiny and further research; and
– What might be the elements of a policy toward the improvement of the present situation, including suggestions for its implementation.

2. Reasonably safe and relevant knowledge related to the present situation

What are the basic facts of the present situation, i.e. what is reasonably safe knowledge that cannot seriously be called in question, and what parts of it are particularly relevant to desirable and possible improvements in the present situation or for the development of a policy plan? The following — inevitably incomplete — list is an attempt to highlight these facts:

AILA Review 20 (2007), 123–133. DOI 10.1075/aila.20.11amm
ISSN 1461–0213 / E-ISSN 1570–5595 © John Benjamins Publishing Company

1. English is the predominantly preferred language of science especially for inter-
    national communication, but it is also making inroads within non-Anglophone
    countries (see e.g. Gill, this volume; Ammon 1998; Carli & Calaresu 2003). English
    is used extensively by non-Anglophone scientists, passively and actively, for writ-
    ten and oral publications (printed materials and conference presentations) as well
    as correspondence (see, e.g. Hamel; Guardiano, Favilla & Calaresu, this volume).

2. The preference for English is much stronger in the pure or theoretical sciences
    than in the applied sciences and especially the humanities (Hamel; Guardiano,
    Favilla & Calaresu, this volume).

3. English can be called the "dominant" language of science because scientists — and
    to a lesser extent scholars in the humanities — are forced to use it if they want to
    follow new developments in their disciplines (passive use) or to be acknowledged
    and make their contributions known beyond their own language community (ac-
    tive use) (Guardiano, Favilla & Calaresu; Gill, this volume).

4. There is, it seems (though reliable data are missing), an asymmetric, Anglophone-
    centered flow of information. Anglophones read publications that are almost
    exclusively in English and preferably from Anglophone countries. Non-Anglo-
    phones do basically the same thing but also read publications in their own lan-
    guages. However, they read relatively few publications in other languages, i.e. the
    communication flow between languages other than English is meager (Hamel,
    this volume).

5. English is the global lingua franca in science (and also in other fields, such as
    economics) but differs from a lingua franca in the narrower sense in that it is, at
    the same time, the native language (or mother tongue) of a substantial subset of
    participants in the communicative process (the Anglophones) (Flowerdew; Gaz-
    zola & Grin; van Parijs, this volume).

6. The existence of a global lingua franca has advantages for everyone, including the
    non-Anglophones and their countries. It also has advantages for the development
    of science in that it enhances international and global cooperation and accelerates
    the spread of new scientific findings (Coulmas, this volume), but the preference of
    a single lingua franca has raised concerns as well (cf. Hamel; Gill, this volume).

7. Naturally, this situation gives the native an advantage over the non-native (or
    foreign-language or English-as-an-additional-language) speakers. Native speak-
    ers have to invest less in language learning, i.e. to contribute less to the creation of
    the public good of a common lingua franca than non-native speakers (Gazzola &
    Grin; van Parijs, this volume). However, as they have a better mastery of the lan-
    guage, this enables them to produce linguistically more refined texts with superior
    impact on the recipients (see, e.g. Flowerdew, this volume).

8. It may be that this linguistic advantage means that native speakers of English also
    more often function as the gatekeepers (reviewers etc.) for important publishing
    institutions like journals or conferences than non-native speakers, i.e. they have

a higher degree of control over scientific outcomes (Flowerdew; Hamel, this volume).

9. As a consequence of the native speakers' linguistic advantage, countries with English as the native language for substantial segments of the population (Anglophone countries) have a competitive advantage in scientific communication over the countries with other linguistic affiliations. They form a linguistically privileged minority in contrast with the underprivileged majority of countries (Gazzola & Grin; van Parijs, this volume). Their communicative advantage encompasses the entire business of science communication and results in higher economic benefits, for example, for publishers.

10. The communicative advantage also translates into the native speakers' and their countries' general advantage in the realm of science. Among other reasons, it contributes, for example, to the Anglophone countries' or their universities' superior share in scientific paradigm building and science awards or in attracting internationally mobile scientists and students (see, e.g. Gazzola & Grin, this volume).

11. The prominence of English in scientific communication further enhances the language's value in use and prestige and increasingly motivates individuals to study and to use it. In a sort of self-supporting, circular process, this also stabilizes its global lingua franca function in fields other than science. The continued expansion of the language's functions further increases the Anglophone individuals' and countries' linguistic advantage but could, in the long run, reduce it if English were to become a basic skill also in the non-Anglophone countries (see, e.g., Hamel, this volume; Graddol 2006: 122 f.).

12. There seems to be incipient awareness among Anglophones as well as among non-Anglophones of the latters' linguistic problems and disadvantages in scientific communication and the growing readiness, in principle, to work towards more fairness (see, e.g., Flowerdew; Guardiano, Favilla & Calaresu this volume).

I can only provide a brief explanation of how the present situation has evolved (for details, see, e.g. Ammon 1998: 179–204). The main, more immediate reasons can be guessed from history and are fairly common knowledge. Roughly speaking, the three languages English, French and German were of similar importance for scientific communication at the beginning of the 20th century, with their countries forming the three main centers of science. As a consequence of WW I, Nazism, WW II, and finally the fall of the Soviet Union, the US rose to the position of a leading world power with dominance in science and today forms the single dominant center and biggest market for science world-wide. As a consequence, its language has become the global lingua franca of science. This process was accelerated and stabilized by more specific processes like the development of representative bibliographical data bases (like *Chemical Abstracts*) or the Citation Indices in the US and by halo effects such as the extension of the prestige of the global scientific center to its language and vice versa.

It should also be pointed out that the rise of English to the preferred language of science was doubtlessly in the interest of the US and other Anglophone countries, which therefore, understandably, promoted it. While criticism of such language policy might seem justified in many respects, those labeling it "linguistic imperialism" should, however, be aware of the following two circumstances:

–   Most countries or language communities also try to promote or spread their own language and would welcome its standing as the world language of science with the accompanying privileges.
–   The effects of direct language promotion as such are usually quite limited. This can be deduced from the fact that competing countries or language communities, for example France and the French-speaking countries, have been at least as eager as the Anglophone countries to promote their language but have been less successful. They lacked the resources and the promise which language promotion needs to be successful, including science, which they were unable to develop on the same scale as the Anglophone countries.

Finally, scholars dealing with the topic should be aware of their own language interests, which tend to coincide with those of their own country or language community, namely to increase their own language's use and value and to defend or raise its national and international standing. They are, consequently, always in danger of being either biased in favour of their own language and its promotion or — where they are aware of the danger — to exaggerate the criticism of their own country's policy.

3.   Open questions that require further research

The "safe knowledge" mentioned previously is of course only relatively safe. However, it is safer, in my opinion, than the following assumptions, which would also be relevant for a policy plan, but which are in greater need of further theoretical foundation and empirical corroboration. These examples of "open questions" are again an incomplete list. Some of them may be less open than I assume because I may have overlooked relevant theoretical approaches or data or even comprehensive answers, in which case I stand ready to be corrected.

1.   It seems clear enough that English is by far the preferred language of science and also of the humanities, but it also seems likely that data usually presented as evidence are often skewed in favor of English as a consequence of the bias towards English in the sources (see, e.g., Hamel, this volume). It would be helpful to know the real proportions of language use and to what extent data on language shares in scientific publications are actually skewed. How much higher (or perhaps even lower) are the actual proportions of languages other than English compared to the data usually presented suggest? A valid and reliable answer to this question

would presumably have to be based on the analysis of a direct, representative global sample of scientific publications instead of available data bases which are, for good reasons, suspected to be skewed towards English. It seems hardly necessary to point out the large scale of such a task, but tackling it might be worth-while to understand the actual roles that languages play in publications.

2. There is a need to understand in which fields would it be worthwhile regularly to read publications in languages other than English, and in which languages it would therefore be worthwhile acquiring reading skills. Or in which fields are languages other than English still used internationally on a regular basis for oral scientific communication, especially at conferences? Quantities of publications or conference use could be a rough guide, but a more reliable guide would of course be based on additional qualitative analyses, which would be much more difficult and would have to be done by experts in each of the respective fields. Reasonably safe knowledge on such a basis could be helpful for scientists' or scholars' decisions regarding language learning and for checking publications and attending conferences. In Germany, the subjects which still use languages other than English for international communication have been termed *niche subjects* ("Nischenfächer", forming niches for these languages), but they have not been studied thoroughly so far (see, e.g. Ammon 1998: 170–178). It seems likely that reasonably reliable knowledge about the scientific value in use of languages other than English exists in many fields and would just have to be collected and made generally available.

3. Another open question seems to be whether the scientific information flow is really as extremely Anglophone-centered as has been widely assumed (see 4 in the previous chapter), seemingly on a largely anecdotal basis. Is it really true that Anglophone scientists have a strong preference for publications of their fellow countrypersons and largely ignore other publications, even if they are written in English? There is some counterevidence (Garfield & Welljams-Dorof 1990), but this question also deserves further scrutiny.

4. Following up such studies, the difficult question that should be tackled is to what extent the Anglophone-centered information flow, if corroborated, would be due primarily to linguistic reasons (distribution of language skills) or to stereotypical perceptions of excellence and established prestige or, justifiably, to superior scientific quality and leadership in paradigm building? Clearly, any valid and reliable attempt at answering this question would be extremely demanding and could probably only be based on a whole series of theoretical as well as empirical studies.

5. A question debated over and again without agreement being reached is whether the single lingua franca enhances or hampers the development of science. This issue has to be divided into at least two questions, of which one will be specified here and the other under 6). It seems clear enough that, as a rule, a single lingua franca saves time and energy for language learning and translation as compared to learning several languages. It also enhances the faster and more complete spread

of knowledge because there are fewer language barriers (the need of only one instead of several translations). Therefore, the reduction from formerly three or even six international languages of science (English, French, German or also Italian, Spanish, and Russian) to only one creates synergies. The savings in time and energy can be used for other purposes, for example for scientific research proper. Reduction to a single lingua franca might have the additional advantage for the non-native users that it enhances the chance of eventually taking control of the language and even setting its norm, since they form a growing majority vis-à-vis the native speakers and can acquire more solid and comprehensive skills than in the case of several languages. Thus, their disadvantage vis-à-vis the native speakers might gradually shrink. For a better evaluation of the present situation, it is highly desirable to scrutinize and specify these potential advantages of a single lingua franca.

6.   An important disadvantage of only one lingua franca in science, the loss of the greater cognitive potential of several languages, has been deplored (Coulmas with a skeptical note and Hamel rather in agreement, both this volume; Ammon 2006: 17 f.). This view has been based on the Humboldt and Whorf hypothesis, which in essence suggests that different languages — because of their different structure, vocabulary and perhaps pragmatic and discourse rules — enhance different knowledge formation or perceptions of reality. Such a possibility has been demonstrated with considerable plausibility in the comparison of selected features for numerous languages. It remains, however, an open question whether such findings based on studies of everyday language can be transferred to the scientific potential of language diversity. I would assume that different cognitive potentials of languages could be of heuristic value, enhancing creativity in finding new research topics and hypotheses, but would be skeptical with respect to their value for theory construction or methodology. For a sounder answer to this complex question, further careful studies seem to be necessary. Then we would be able to judge more safely the potential respective disadvantages of a single lingua franca of science.

Whatever the final answer to that question may be, a single lingua franca of science should by no means be equaled with world-wide monolingualism in scientific communication, since non-Anglophones can of course continue to use their native tongue on the national level in addition to English. And if the Humboldt and Whorf hypothesis were confirmed to be true and applicable to science, this would support the non-Anglophones' position. This is because it would prove that they are linguistically better equipped for being scientifically creative, being bi- or multilingual (at least their own language + English) than their Anglophone competitors, who are blindfolded by their monolingualism.

7.   The advantages of only a single lingua franca outlined under 5) are especially noticeable for the scientists or communities whose languages have always been excluded from international scientific communication. However, for those scientists

whose language was until recently also used for international scientific communication, the reduction to the use of only English has created a loss in convenience, influence and prestige. It is therefore not astonishing that criticism of the "dominance" of English has been raised mostly from their side (e.g. Durand 2001 from the French perspective). It would be useful to study the special hardships and frustrations these scientists experience in comparison to their happier peers of smaller languages like, for example, Dutch or Greek, to better understand their case and to find a fairer solution for them as well.

8. Another problem worth studying is the extra burden for scientists of languages with a great linguistic distance from English as compared to those who know related languages. Comparative studies of learning times and other difficulties have been done (cf., e.g. Chong 2003) and would be worthwhile collecting and examining in detail. They are proof that it is much harder, for example, for East Asians than for most Europeans, especially those of a Germanic linguistic background, to acquire solid skills in English, which corresponds to observations that are easy to make in international encounters. The more thorough knowledge of these differences would be helpful in designing a language policy that worked towards more fairness in international scientific communication.

9. Although it seems clear that a financial compensation for linguistic advantages cannot seriously be expected from the Anglophone countries, it seems worthwhile to try to figure out what would be a justifiable amount, following the two studies in this volume that touch on or deal with the question, though from different frameworks and on different levels of abstraction (Gazzola & Grin; van Parijs). The ability to argue on the basis of careful economic analysis could help to set up an adequate perspective for a language policy plan. It could also be useful for finding other possibilities for compensation, if possible and if compensation could convincingly be shown to be justified, beyond van Parijs' interesting proposal of "poaching" the Internet (this volume).

10. Finally, with respect to future development, it would be worthwhile to reexamine Graddol's prediction (2006: 122 f.; also Hamel, this volume) that the Anglophones' linguistic advantage will eventually shrink as English becomes a global basic skill. The scenarios to be analyzed in such a study should also be useful for assessing the non-native speakers' chances of acquiring language skills equivalent, for scientific purposes, to those of the native speakers and even of managing to break the natives' normative control of the language (see point 5). This would mean for British English, for example, that it would no longer be more correct than, let's say, Chinese English, about whose correctness China and not any Anglophone country would have to decide. Thus, English might become a new, autonomous, multi-centric global language whatever its name may ultimately be (e.g. "Globalish" or "Globish") (Ammon 2006: 25 f.). Studies of the possibility of such a development are highly desirable with respect to a long-term language policy perspective. If such a scenario ever became reality, it would certainly go a

long way towards silencing all complaints about linguistic disadvantages in scientific communication.

4. Policy suggestions

The following suggestions are very preliminary indeed and aim at getting planning started rather than at presenting actual plans (cf. Ammon 2001: vii f.; 2006: 21–27). Any policy should be guided by the principles which are explicated in Gazzola & Grin's and in van Parijs' contributions to this volume, namely that it should improve fairness in sharing the burden among participants in scientific communication of different linguistic affiliation without diminishing efficiency.

1. The issue to start with would be an awareness campaign, i.e. publicizing the problem as widely as possible (an example is La Madeleine's article in *Nature*, 2007). Such campaigns could, in some respects, resemble those against gender discrimination through language and language use, although the present issue is quite different in nature and, presumably, more difficult to resolve. The most appropriate and qualified agents to kick off such a campaign would be linguistic organizations. They could use their periodicals for that purpose, as AILA does with this volume, and their conferences, as AILA should its World Congress 2008 in Essen. Proposals of similar actions should be sent to other linguistic and non-linguistic scientific organizations. It might be useful to establish committees at the various organizations, starting with at AILA, for planning and carrying out such activities. These committees should try to conceive possible improvements like the following, which need further analysis and testing for feasibility, and to develop agendas of how to proceed.

2. Anglophone speakers at international conferences should be sensitized to the possibility that non-Anglophone participants might have difficulty following their oral contributions if they presented them as they would be normal audience of native speakers. They should be encouraged to try a slower pace and to be more careful with pronunciation as in "foreigner talk" and, in addition, to rephrase more complex passages. There is, of course, always the danger of tediousness in such an attempt. Practicable guideless may, however, help to avoid that.

3. There should be more translation and interpretation made available for conference participants who are unable to make their contributions in English. It should be possible to present papers in a number of other major languages, which would have to be specified, and to have them translated or interpreted. Such services are of course costly but could be made affordable by limiting their extent and by financing them through (slightly) increased conference fees and additional financial contributions by those who benefit from them. These services would also

require reviewing the contributions in the original language to guarantee quality of content, which might prove to be difficult to organize.

4. More editorial support for non-Anglophones who are unable to write scientific English is another urgent desideratum. Such support is presently available informally, e.g. by peers for those who are lucky, as well as by professional specialists (Burrough-Boenisch 2006). The latter is, however, expensive. Any form of editorial support can require intensive interaction between the author and the aid or translator (Flowerdew, this volume). Scientific organizations and publishers should think about possible ways to provide assistance. Clearly, support from a scientific organization would be difficult to organize because, for one reason among others, papers would again have to be reviewed for quality of content beforehand. The committees entrusted with the problem should, however, be able to draw up some practicable improvement. A number of journals try to deal with the problem through the use of language editors.

5. For a more comprehensive support, better systematic training of non-Anglophones in writing scientific texts would be highly desirable. Presently, possibilities are very limited even at otherwise well-equipped tertiary or research institutions (cf. Murray & Dingwall 1997; Flowerdew, this volume). Committees could develop recommendations for improvements to be published and distributed to institutions.

6. Practical proposals as presented so far should be expanded by critical components as suggested by Flowerdew (this volume) in what he calls a "critical pragmatic approach". The awareness campaign (suggestion 1) should involve such critical components right away. The more demanding of these components may have a somewhat utopian overtone but should, nevertheless, be carefully examined as to their feasibility. One of them is the request for more language norm tolerance vis-à-vis non-native speakers or, as I have phrased it, "the non-native speakers' right to linguistic peculiarities" (Ammon 2003). This request is often immediately rejected by depicting the dangers of "everything goes" and communicative chaos or the extra burden native speakers would have to bear in such communication. It seems indeed very difficult to specify acceptability beyond native norms that still guarantees communication (Burrough-Boenisch 2006). But it is also obvious that there are numerous non-native features that do not seriously hinder communication. The comprehensive studies of "English as a lingua franca" published in the meantime (e.g. Knapp & Meierkord 2002) provide ample proof of that. They should be used for encouraging the acceptance of non-native forms to a much greater extent than today and to motivate editors and publishers to consider them accordingly. I am not sure however, to what extent they could also be used for defining limits of acceptability without being unnecessarily restrictive.

7. A related task would be planning to institutionalize and to put to practice "International English", which has been studied intensively in recent years (Seidlhofer 2003, among several other scholars). I would personally prefer a still more com-

prehensive approach, which should at the same time be even fairer and more acceptable for non-Anglophones. It may seem forbiddingly utopian but is, in my view, not impossible to become true in the long run. One could even argue that essential components of it are already a reality today. This approach would be to develop or encourage the development of a new, autonomous language (Ammon 2003: 33 f.; 2006: 25 f.; Chapter 3 above: point 10), perhaps on the basis of International English. To underline its autonomy, which would make it more acceptable to non-Anglophones and reduce its colonial and imperial package, it should be renamed "Globalish" or a similar term, avoiding the allusion to "English". It ought to be conceived as a multi-centric, global language, according to the model of symmetric pluricentric languages (cf. Clyne 1992), i.e. with centers having principally the same rights to the language and their own French, Japanese, British etc. varieties, all of which would be accepted as equally correct. National institutes would have to do the planning and codification of their own varieties and cooperate globally in keeping the language from drifting apart to guarantee the functioning of communication. Continuing technical progress, enhancing ever more intensive global communication, would probably go a long way towards holding the numerous varieties together. Communication would be possible because of sufficient linguistic similarity of varieties, and national identity would be able to be expressed through their specific features at the same time. Unfortunately, there is no space here to go into more detail. But I hope that the idea of such a global language may be appealing enough to seriously think about its feasibility and to try to evaluate its advantages and disadvantages. It would be an extremely complex task, which would require ample time and resources to accomplish, but one which, in my view, would certainly be worth tackling. It should in any case be discussed by linguistic committees that would need to examine these proposals.

References

Ammon, U. 1998. *Ist Deutsch noch internationale Wissenschaftssprache? Englisch auch für die Lehre an den deutschsprachigen Hochschulen.* Berlin: Walter de Gruyter.

Ammon, U. (ed.). 2001. *The Dominance of English as a Language of Science. Effects on other languages and language communities.* Berlin: Mouton de Gruyter.

Ammon, U. (2003) Global English and the non-native speaker: Overcoming disadvantage. In *Language in the 21st Century*, H. Tonkin & T. Reagan (eds), 23–34. Amsterdam: John Benjamins.

Ammon, U. 2006. Language planning for international scientific communication: An overview of questions and potential solutions *Current Issues in Language Planning* 7(1): 1–30.

Burrough-Boenisch, J. 2006. Negotiable acceptability: Reflections on the interactions between language professionals in Europe and NSS scientists wishing to publish in English. *Current Issues in Language Planning* 7(1): 31–43.

Carli, A. & Calaresu, E. 2003. Le lingua della comunicazione scientifica. La producione e la diffusione des sapere specialistico in Italia. In *Ecologia Linguistica*, A. Valentini et al. (eds.), 27–74. Rome: Bulzoni.

Chong, Si-Ho. 2003. Gründe für die größere Attraktivität von Englisch, Japanisch und Chinesisch als Deutsch in Korea. In *Die deutsche Sprache in Korea*, U. Ammon & S.-I. Chong (eds), 297–315. München: Iudicium.

Clyne, M. (ed.). 1992. *Pluricentric Languages. Differing Norms in Differing Nations*. Berlin & New York: Mouton de Gruyter.

Garfield, E. & Welljams-Dorof, A. 1990. Language use in international research. A citation analysis. *Annals of the American Academy of Political and Social Science* 511: 10–24.

Durand, C. 2001. *La mise en place des monopoles du savoir*. Paris: L'Harmattan.

Graddol, D. 2006 *English Next. Why global English may mean the end of 'English as a Foreign Language'*. London: British Council.

Knapp, K. & Meierkord, C. (eds). 2002. *Lingua Franca Communication*. Frankfurt: Peter Lang.

La Madeleine, B.L. 2007. Lost in translation. English is the language of science. So to what extent are researchers who are non-native English speakers at a disadvantage? *Nature* 445: 454 f.

Murray, H. & Dingwall, S. 1997. English for scientific communication at Swiss universities: 'God helps those who help themselves'. *Babylonia* 4: 54–59.

Seidlhofer, B. 2003. *A Concept of International English and Related Issues: From 'Real English' to 'Realistic English'*. Strasbourg: Council of Europe.

Access to online full text

Ingenta *connect*

John Benjamins Publishing Company's journals are available in online full-text format as of the volume published in 2000. Some of our journals have additional (multi-media) information available that is referred to in the articles.

Access to the electronic edition of a volume is included in your subscription. We offer a pay-per-view service per article for those journals and volumes to which you did not subscribe.

Full text is provided in PDF. In order to read these documents you will need Adobe Acrobat Reader, which is freely available from **www.adobe.com/products/ acrobat/readstep2.html**

You can access the electronic edition through the gateways of major subscription agents (SwetsWise, EBSCO EJS, Maruzen) or directly through IngentaConnect.

If you currently use **www.ingenta.com** or **www.ingentaselect.com** (formely, Catchword) to access your subscriptions, these rights have been carried over to **www. ingentaconnect.com**, the new, fully merged service. All bookmarked pages will also be diverted to the relevant pages on **www.ingentaconnect.com**.

If you have not yet set up access to the electronic version of the journal at IngentaConnect, please follow these instructions:

If you are a personal subscriber:
- Register free at **www.ingentaconnect.com**. This is a one-time process, that provides IngentaConnect with the information they need to be able to match your data with the subscription data provide by the publisher. Your registration also allows you to use the e-mail alerting services.
- Select *Personal subscriptions.*
- Select the publication title and enter your subscription number. Your subscription number can be found on the shipping label with the print journal, and on the invoice/renewal invitation.
- You will be notified by email once your online access has been activated.

If you are an institutional subscriber:
- Register free at **www.ingentaconnect.com** by selecting the registration link and following the link to institutional registration.
- Select *Set up subscriptions.*
- Select the publication title and enter your subscription number. Your subscription number can be found on the shipping label with the print journal, and on the invoice/renewal invitation.
- You will be notified by email once your online access has been activated.
  If you purchase subscriptions via a subscription agent they will be able to set up subscriptions on IngentaConnect on your behalf – simply pass them your IngentaConnect ID, sent to you at registration.

If you would like further information or assistance with your registration, please contact **help@ingentaconnect.com**.

For information on our journals, please visit **www.benjamins.com**

New in Applied Linguistics

Discourse in *Content and Language Integrated Learning* (CLIL) Classrooms

Christiane Dalton-Puffer

University of Vienna

The label CLIL stands for classrooms where a foreign language (English) is used as a medium of instruction in content subjects. This book provides a first in-depth analysis of the kind of communicative abilities which are embodied in such CLIL classrooms. It examines teacher and student talk at secondary school level from different discourse-analytic angles, taking into account the interpersonal pragmatics of classroom discourse and how school subjects are talked into being during lessons. The analysis shows how CLIL classroom interaction is strongly shaped by its institutional context, which in turn conditions the ways in which students experience, use and learn the target language. The research presented here suggests that CLIL programmes require more explicit language learning goals in order to fully exploit their potential for furthering the learners' appropriation of a foreign language as a medium of learning.

[Language Learning & Language Teaching, 20] 2007. xii, 330 pp.

HB   978 90 272 1979 4 EUR 110.00 / USD 149.00
PB   978 90 272 1981 7 EUR 36.00 / USD 48.95

French Applied Linguistics

Edited by Dalila Ayoun

University of Arizona

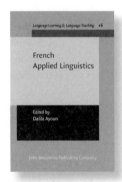

This state-of-the-art volume on French Applied Linguistics includes two introductory chapters, the first summarizes the past, present and future of French in applied linguistics, and the second reviews the history of French from a sociolinguistic perspective. The six chapters of the first part cover the core aspects of the second language acquisition of French: phonology, semantics/syntax, syntax/morphology, pragmatics, sociolinguistics, and grammatical gender. The seven chapters of the second part explore the contribution of French in various subfields of applied linguistics such as language ideology and foreign language pedagogy, corpus linguistics, and French Sign Language. A chapter studies the role of affective variables on language learning, while another investigates natural language and lexical creativity. The chapters on creole studies and applied linguistics in West Africa address issues in first and second language acquisition in complex sociolinguistic and political contexts. The last chapter serves as an epilogue focusing on Louisiana, a region rich in linguistic history.

[Language Learning & Language Teaching, 16] 2007. xvi, 560 pp.

HB   978 90 272 1972 5 EUR 130.00 / USD 176.00

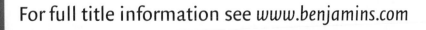

For full title information see *www.benjamins.com*

New in Applied Linguistics

Language Experience in Second Language Speech Learning

In honor of James Emil Flege

Edited by Ocke-Schwen Bohn and Murray J. Munro

Aarhus University / Simon Fraser University

This stimulating collection of articles from leading international researchers provides a state-of-the-art overview of core issues in second language speech perception and production. Aimed at phoneticians, speech scientists, psycholinguists, applied linguists, and pedagogical specialists, it presents engaging discussions of fundamental problems and controversies within the field, as well as new empirical findings arising from a variety of methodological approaches. Its twenty chapters, inspired by the ground-breaking work of James E. Flege, address such topics as the theoretical underpinnings of second language speech learning; the nature and etiology of foreign accents; the effects of age, experience, and training; speech intelligibility; and the acquisition of vowels, consonants, tone, and prosody. This volume will serve as a valuable resource, not only for researchers, but for anyone wishing to gain an understanding of an area of linguistics that is rapidly growing in importance.

[Language Learning & Language Teaching, 17] 2007. xvii, 406 pp.
HB 978 90 272 1973 2 EUR 115.00 / USD 155.00

Learner and Teacher Autonomy

Concepts, realities, and responses

Edited by Terry Lamb and Hayo Reinders

University of Sheffield / Department of Second Language Studies, University of Hawaii

This edited volume offers a cohesive account of recent developments across the world in the field of learner and teacher autonomy in languages education. Drawing on the work of eminent researchers of language learning and teaching, it explores at both conceptual and practical levels issues related to current pedagogical developments in a wide range of contexts. Global shifts have led to an increase in autonomous and independent learning both in policy and practice (including self-access and distance learning). The book's scope and focus will therefore be beneficial to language teachers as well as to students and researchers in applied linguistics and those involved in pre- and in-service teacher education. The book concludes with an overview of the state of research in this field, focusing on the (inter)relationships between the concepts of learner and teacher autonomy.

[AILA Applied Linguistics Series, 1] 2008. vii, 286 pp.
HB 978 90 272 0517 9 EUR 99.00 / USD 134.00

For full title information see *www.benjamins.com*

New in Applied Linguistics

Learning and Teaching Languages Through Content
A counterbalanced approach

Roy Lyster
McGill University

Based on a synthesis of classroom SLA research that has helped to shape evolving perspectives of content-based instruction since the introduction of immersion programs in Montreal more than 40 years ago, this book presents an updated perspective on integrating language and content in ways that engage second language learners with language across the curriculum. A range of instructional practices observed in immersion and content-based classrooms is highlighted to set the stage for justifying a counterbalanced approach that integrates both content-based and form-focused instructional options as complementary ways of intervening to develop a learner's interlanguage system. A counterbalanced approach is outlined as an array of opportunities for learners to process language through content by means of comprehension, awareness, and production mechanisms, and to negotiate language through content by means of interactional strategies involving teacher scaffolding and feedback.

[Language Learning & Language Teaching, 18] 2007. xii, 173 pp.
HB   978 90 272 1974 9 EUR 105.00 / USD 142.00
PB   978 90 272 1976 3 EUR   33.00 / USD   44.95

Literacies, Global and Local
Edited by Mastin Prinsloo and Mike Baynham
University of Cape Town / University of Leeds

The articles collected in this volume draw on or relate to a body of work that has become known as the 'New Literacy Studies' (NLS), which studies literacy as situated semiotic practices that vary across sites in specific ways that are socially shaped. The collection offers a body of empirically and theoretically based papers on literacy ethnography as well as providing engagements with critical issues around literacy and education. The articles offer complementary perspectives on research and theory in literacy studies and include research perspectives from Africa, Asia, Australia, Europe, as well as North and South America. The researchers are all concerned to take the work of the New Literacy Studies further by expanding on its conceptual resources and research sites.

[AILA Applied Linguistics Series, 2] 2008. vii, 213 pp. + index
HB   978 90 272 0518 6 EUR 95.00 / USD 128.00
Expected April 2008

For full title information see *www.benjamins.com*

New in Applied Linguistics

Mediating Discourse Online

Edited by Sally Sieloff Magnan

University of Wisconsin, Madison

Information and communication technology is transforming our notion of literacy. In the study of second language learning, there is an acute need to understand how learners collaborate in mediating discourse online. This edited volume offers essays and research studies that lead us to question the borders between speech and writing, to redefine narrative, to speculate on the consequences of many-to-many communication, and to ponder the ethics of researching online interaction. Using diverse technologies (bulletin boards, course management systems, chats, instant messaging, online gaming) and situated in different cultural environments, the studies explore intercultural notions of identity, voice, and collaboration. Although the studies come from varying theoretical perspectives, they point, as a whole, to insights to be gained from an ecological approach to studying how people make discourse online. The volume will especially benefit researchers in the digital arena and instructors who must consider how online interaction affects language learning and use.

[AILA Applied Linguistics Series, 3] 2008. vii, 355 pp. + index

HB 978 90 272 0519 3 EUR 105.00 / USD 142.00

Expected April 2008

Memory, Psychology and Second Language Learning

Mick Randall

British University in Dubai

This book explores the contributions that cognitive linguistics and psychology, including neuropsychology, have made to the understanding of the way that second languages are processed and learnt. It examines areas of phonology, word recognition and semantics, examining 'bottom-up' decoding processes as compared with 'top-down' processes as they affect memory. It also discusses second language learning from the acquisition/learning and nativist/connectionist perspectives. These ideas are then related to the methods that are used to teach second languages, primarily English, in formal classroom situations. This examination involves both 'mainstream' communicative approaches, and more traditional methods widely used to teach EFL throughout the world. The book is intended to act both as a textbook for students who are studying second language teaching and as an exploration of issues for the interested teacher who would like to further extend their understanding of the cognitive processes underlying their teaching.

Mick Randall is currently Senior Lecturer in TESOL and Head of the Institute of Education at the British University in Dubai. He has taught courses in second language learning and teaching, applied linguistics and psychology in a number of different contexts. He has a special interest in the cognitive processing of language and in the psycholinguistics of word recognition, spelling and reading.

[Language Learning & Language Teaching, 19] 2007. x, 220 pp.

HB 978 90 272 1977 0 EUR 105.00 / USD 142.00
PB 978 90 272 1978 7 EUR 36.00 / USD 48.95

For full title information see *www.benjamins.com*

Phraseology

An interdisciplinary perspective

Edited by Sylviane Granger and Fanny Meunier

Université catholique de Louvain, Belgium

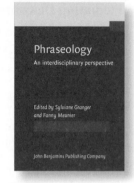

Long regarded as a peripheral issue, phraseology is now taking
centre stage in a wide range of fields. This recent explosion of
interest undoubtedly has a great deal to do with the development
of corpus linguistics research, which has both demonstrated
the key role of phraseological expressions in language and
provided researchers with automated methods of extraction
and analysis. The aim of this volume is to take stock of current
research in phraseology from a variety of perspectives: theoretical, descriptive,
contrastive, cultural, lexicographic and computational. It contains overview chapters
by leading experts in the field and a series of case studies focusing on a wide range of
multiword units: collocations, similes, idioms, routine formulae and recurrent phrases.
The volume is an invitation for experienced phraseologists to look at the field with
different eyes and a useful introduction for the many researchers who are intrigued
by phraseology but need help in finding their way in this rich but complex domain.

2008. xxviii, 412 pp. + index

HB 978 90 272 3246 5 EUR 125.00 / USD 169.00

Expected May 2008